MW00973534

GOD:
HE IS WHO HE IS

A 40-Day Journey towards Knowing the True God

Marty Williamson, a Non-Theologian Who
Has Come to Know God More Closely,
And by
Rev. Bobby Linkous, Pastor of
Shadowbrook Baptist Church
Suwanee, Georgia

Xulon PRESS

God: He Is Who He Is
A 40-Day Journey towards Knowing the True God
by Marty Williamson and Rev. Bobby Linkous

Printed in the United States of America

ISBN 978-1-60266-943-7

www.xulonpress.com

Sermon Packages

Pastor Bobby Linkous of Shadowbrook Baptist Church has developed a package that contains a four-sermon series that complements the 40-day study. In addition, there are three simple skits that can be performed by a member of your church that are excellent supplements to the sermons.

Ordering Sermon Package and Obtaining Volume Discount

For information on how to order copies of the sermon / skit package or for information on how to obtain volume discount pricing for the 40-day study, please contact Shadowbrook Baptist Church at:

Shadowbrook Baptist Church
4187 Suwanee Dam Road
Suwanee, GA 30024
(770) 945-1524
www.shadowbrookchurch.org

"What comes into our minds when we think about God is the most important thing about us." A. W. Tozer

"Be advised. You are entering holy ground. You are welcome to tread here, but do so attentively. The study of God himself is the loftiest and most significant pursuit that you could ever undertake." Chip Ingram

"Disregard the study of God, and you sentence yourself to stumble and blunder through life blindfolded, as it were, with no sense of direction and no understanding of what surrounds you. This way you can waste your life and lose your soul." J. I. Packer

"When we don't see him (God) with 20/20 vision, it distorts every other area of our lives." Chip Ingram

"Without doubt, the mightiest thought the mind can entertain is the thought of God." A. W. Tozer

"The essence of idolatry is the entertainment of thoughts about God that are unworthy of Him." A. W. Tozer

"The highest science, the loftiest speculation, the mightiest philosophy, which can ever engage the attention of a child of God, is the name, the nature, the person, the work, the doings, and the existence of the great God whom he calls father." J. I. Packer

"Now devote your heart and soul to seeking the Lord your God." King David (1 Chronicles 22:19)

GOD: HE IS WHO HE IS

Our Goals

Our goals for this forty day study are that you will better know and understand the true God and will start to build that deep, personal relationship with God that will carry you through the rest of your life.

We want you to see God in all of His majesty. However, we also want you to know, with complete confidence, that God desires a special, intimate relationship with you – one where you are His child and He is your heavenly Daddy. Finally, our hope is that your knowledge of God will create a desire in you to be more Christ-like.

Our Approach

A study about God can be seen by some as too theologically deep, but our hope is that you will see this as one of the most important things you will do. We have attempted to create an easy-to-read, 40-day study guide about God. We readily admit that many of the thoughts expressed come from some great theologians and authors. If you would like to engage in a deeper, theological study, we highly recommend the books from which much of this 40-day journey is based:

1. The Knowledge of the Holy, by A. W. Tozer
2. God: As He Longs for You To See Him, by Chip Ingram
3. Knowing God, by J. I. Packer

This study is written for any Christian – from the beginner to the knowledgeable. Our approach is to:
- discuss the importance of truly knowing God
- describe some of the key attributes of God
- examine how Jesus portrayed God to us
- provide some real examples of how God's attributes have been made evident, and
- identify how we can apply our knowledge of God in our lives.

Each day we will address "The What" and the "So What?" regarding that daily topic. "The What" will be an explanation of the topic for the day, and the "So What?" will bring application of the topic to your daily life. Hopefully, during the rest of the day, you will think about what you have read. Maybe you will even have one of those "Aha!" moments when you can relate the message to something specific in your life that day.

Preface

Take a moment to reflect on these four questions:

1. Do you know the one true God as described in the Bible?
2. What kind of thoughts do you have about God?
3. What kind of a relationship do you have with the almighty God?
4. Do your knowledge, thoughts and relationship affect the way you live your life?

These are important questions; but for most of us, they are difficult to confidently and precisely answer. However, make no mistake; what you know and think about God will affect how you live and will determine where you focus your time, energy and resources.

Remember in the movie "City Slickers" when Curly (Jack Palance) held up one finger and told Mitch (Billy Crystal) that the key to life is finding out what the most important thing in your life is and focusing on that. That is actually a pretty profound statement. What is the number one thing in your life? You? Your spouse? Your family? Sports? Having fun? Your job? Money? Cars, house, clothes, electronics, stuff? Your friends? School? Partying? Once you know the true God, maybe you will want to hold up that index finger and point to God as number one in your life.

So exactly who is our God? In Exodus 3:14, God is speaking to Moses and says: **"I AM WHO I AM**. This is what you are to say to the Israelites: I AM has sent me to you." What does this mean? That statement from God probably has more meaning than we can comprehend. To you and me, one meaning should be: **"HE IS WHO HE IS"**, not who man says He is. Man cannot define God as he wants him to be. WHO HE IS is what this 40-day journey is all about.

As you take this journey, make the effort not just to read the material; but take the time and expend the energy to dwell on God. Ask the Holy Spirit to counsel you, to help you draw near to God, and to know God as you have never known Him before. Perhaps we will all better understand how great and awesome our God is. Now as you begin the journey and each day as you dwell on your heavenly Father, remember what He said:

"Be still, and <u>know</u> that I am God" (Psalm 46:10 NIV)

Table of Contents

Why Should I Make the Effort to Truly Know God?

Day 1 – Introduction

The What

The atheist, evolutionist philosopher Thomas Huxley referred to God as the "eternal unknown". (1) Perhaps this was true for him – but this is definitely not true for the children of God. We can know Him; and, most importantly, He wants us to know Him.

> **This is what the Lord says: "Let not the wise man boast of his wisdom or the strong man boast of his strength or the rich man boast of his riches, but let him who boasts boast about this: <u>that he understands and knows me</u>, that I am the Lord, who exercises kindness, justice and righteousness on earth, for in these I delight," declares the Lord. (Jeremiah 9:23-24 NIV)**

Can you boast that you know and understand the Lord God?

In the office where I used to work someone hung a picture on a wall near our department printer. For two or three weeks I passed by the picture without paying it much attention. The picture simply looked like a pattern of colors to me. Then several of my co-workers told me the picture was an optical illusion and that I needed to stand a few feet from it and stare at it. I was told an image of a city would appear. When I couldn't see the image they were describing, I thought that they were playing a practical joke on me. (It would not have been the first time.) Finally, after a few days and several attempts, the image of the city appeared. It was as if I were looking down on the city from above. I could see the tops of the buildings, streets and cars. I even saw a swimming pool on the top of one building and a helicopter on the top of another. Over time I got to where I could stop in front of the picture and within seconds see the image clearly and with all the details.

What I had learned was that I had to totally focus on the whole picture and not allow other thoughts to enter into my mind. I could not look at a corner or at a specific part of the image, and I could not just take a quick glance and expect to see the image. I had to absorb myself in the image as a whole and then I could start to see and relate specific details.

That is how you need to look at God. You cannot focus on one attribute or characteristic of God and ignore the others. You will never see and understand the true God as He truly is. You need to absorb yourself into seeing and knowing God and you must see the whole picture of God. That, in essence, is the intent of this study – getting to know and understand God more completely.

Keep in mind that you can read the Bible many times over, read Christian books, attend Bible Study regularly and perhaps never really know God. You may know a lot *about* God but you may not know *of* God in a deep, personal way. God longs for us to seek Him, to come to Him, to love Him and to have a personal relationship with Him. Reading the material in this booklet will help you know more about God; however, our desire is that you do more than just read. Take this opportunity to deepen your personal relationship with God through meditation and earnest prayer. Make it a habit to reflect on God throughout your day. This study should be just one step in a life-long journey – a journey whose goal is to truly know the one, true God.

So What?

The outcome of this journey, hopefully, will be reflected in the evidence that you have come to truly know God. Chip Ingram states that once you see God in the proper light, "it will change the way you pray, the way you live, and the way you think about the world around you." (2)

In his classic book, <u>Knowing God</u>, the great theologian J. I. Packer wrote:

1. "Those who know God have great energy for God.
2. Those who know God have great thoughts of God.
3. Those who know God have great boldness for God.
4. Those who know God have great contentment in God." (3)

You will know that God loves you and wants the best for you. You will not underestimate God and will confidently put your trust in Him. You will know that God has the power to deliver on His –promises to you and that He will deliver on His promises to you. You will be content in knowing that you will be blessed eternally by God. Service to God will become a pleasure. You will pray more often and with more conviction, knowing that God is listening. Standing firm in your faith will become easier. Witnessing will become less daunting. Truly knowing the true God is something you will be able to boast about. Think about how we as individuals, as well as your church, can benefit once these results are realized.

One other key point that you should take with you from this study is that you can rest assured that He knows you. What a mind-boggling thought! But what is even more mind-boggling is that He knows you, even at your worst, and still loves you.

Selected Scripture
Proverbs 9:10   1 Corinthians 8:3   1 John 3:1   2 Peter 1:3-8

Prayer
Tell God that you are going to seek Him.
Ask the Holy Spirit to help you draw near to God.
Tell God you want to have a deep, personal, lasting relationship with Him.
Pray that this study will result in great, spiritual blessings for you and for your church.
Be still and listen.

Day 2 – Why Is It Important to Truly Know God?

"What comes into our minds when we think about God is the most important thing about us." A. W. Tozer (1)

The What

The statement above speaks of a truth that all of us live out in our lives every day. When we see God for who He really is, our life will demonstrate it in our actions and thoughts. But when we fail to see God for who He really is, it also has a profound affect on our life. Let's look at a few examples:

1. Some people perceive God to be either too "small" or too "big" to know or care about individual people. God may be viewed as being limited in His powers, so He cannot possibly relate to people on an individual basis. On the other hand, many view God as being so powerful that mankind is rendered unimportant in the overall universe. To them, God is an impersonal "force". Either perception can lead to justification for not getting to know God or having a personal relationship with Him.

2. Some people perceive Him to be "grandpa god". Their perception is that God is too loving and kind to judge and

punish people; so obedience is optional, and rules are flexible. All people are in God's family and will not get booted out unless they are really bad people.

3. Some people do not believe in God, so the only limitations on behavior are what society and government define. God is never a consideration in decisions or actions. There are no absolute rights and wrongs. Values and morals can change over time.

4. Some people have not taken the time to know God, so God is not the chief priority in their lives. These people might focus on personal freedom, accomplishments, wealth, power or pleasure. In Matthew 6:21 Jesus addressed this very concern: **"For where your treasure is, there your heart will be also." (Matthew 6:21)**

5. Some people are scared to get too close to God, because they are afraid of the commitment it might require. (For many years I fell into this category.) These people walk that fine line between committing to God and living for the enjoyment offered by the secular world. For these people, a part-time relationship with God and a partial commitment to God allow them to maintain that satisfactory balance between guilt and fun.

6. Another example are people who believe that you cannot really know God. These people believe in God, but they also believe knowing God is virtually impossible. These people maintain a relationship with God - but at a distance. They do not enjoy all of the benefits of truly knowing God and having a close relationship with Him.

Certainly there are other examples that we could mention. The point is that no matter where you fall right now in your thoughts about God, by the end of this study we want you to feel that you can know God and have a personal relationship with Him. We want each of you to have correct thoughts and great thoughts about God.

Finally, remember that God desires for you to know Him.

For I desired mercy, and not sacrifice; and the knowledge of God more than burnt offerings. (Hosea 6:6 KJV)

Jesus quoted this Old Testament Scripture when talking to the Pharisees. Basically Jesus was saying that knowing and loving God is more important than religiosity.

So What?

Make knowing God a priority. Chip Ingram states: "This is serious business. Nothing in all your life will impact your relationship with God, your relationship with people, your self-view, your decisions, and your purpose like the way you think of God. Everything in you life consciously or unconsciously comes back to one thing: Whom do you visualize God to be in your heart? Who we are and what we become cannot be separated from our understanding of God." (2)

Make knowing God a lifetime goal, and strive to make progress towards that goal every day. Never fall into the trap of being satisfied with what you know about God. Put His Spirit and His Holy Word to work in you daily, and watch as your knowledge and understanding of God increase.

Make having a close, personal relationship to God the most important thing in your life. Your love for God will allow you to truly know Him. I like how Chip Ingram puts it: "In fact, his *revelation* to you will depend largely on his *relationship* to you." (3) A close relationship with God will result in the fullness of the Holy Spirit dwelling within you, and the Holy Spirit is essential for revelation of truth about God and for daily guidance in your life.

Make your daily life reflect your understanding and love for God. Don't just talk the talk, walk the walk. That is why it is important for you to truly know God.

Selected Scripture

1 Corinthians 2:10-16   John 17:3   John 17:25-26
1 John 2:3-6, 3:6

Prayer

If you feel that you have not made the effort to know and understand God, ask for His forgiveness. Tell Him that you want to know Him.

Ask the Holy Spirit for revelation and counsel so that your knowledge and understanding of God will grow.

Pray for the church to grow in its understanding and relationship with God. Pray that your church will have great thoughts of God.

Day 3 – Problems with "Custom-Ordered Gods"

The What

M any people believe in a god of their own choosing. Theirs is a custom, made-to-order god. Let's use the example of ordering a sandwich at a Subway restaurant. When a person orders a sandwich at Subway, he/she chooses the bread, meat, vegetables, ingredients, and toppings they desire and ignore the ones that do not appeal to him/her. Sometimes a person may like onions, but sometimes onions do not appeal to their appetite that day. The sandwich content may differ from one Subway trip to another. Some will even vary their sandwich based on what someone else recommends.

In the same way, the "Subway sandwich" spiritualists create their own custom, sandwich god by picking and choosing beliefs that appeal to them from a variety of religions. When it comes to defining their god, this person will examine the available attributes for a god, much like a person would pick and choose items to make a sandwich. Their god is defined as who they say he is, probably wise, benevolent, good and loving. "Subway sandwich" spiritualists believe their god accepts most religions, because everyone's god is personal to them. Unfortunately for them, this thinking violates God's second commandment of creating an idol, or false god. What these people have done is create a god in their own image.

Even Christians can have some misconceptions of God. Sometimes these misconceptions are just misunderstandings. Other times the misconceptions can come from not truly knowing what God has told us about Himself in the Bible. Although God has not told us everything about Himself, He has revealed enough so that we can know Him if we will take the time to study and meditate on His Word and spend time in earnest prayer.

There is great danger in coming up with our own "version" of whom we believe God is. For example, if you believe only in a god who is only good and loving, one may falsely conclude such beliefs as:

- If my good works outweigh my bad deeds, then I should make it to heaven.
- I'm a "good" person, so I will go to Heaven.
- My god is a loving god and will not send people to hell unless they are just really bad, evil people.

This line of thinking is not Biblically based. In addition, it presents some logical problems - problems that can be bad for you as an individual or bad for society. Consider the problems that can come from a belief that is based on less than a full picture of God and how He relates to mankind:

1. What is the measuring stick for "goodness" and who does the measuring? Is man the standard, or does God set the standard? Man's standards will vary over time, and there will be no absolute truths - no absolute rights and wrongs. "Good" is defined by your culture and times, not by an unchanging God. Is that logical? It's logical if God changes to fit man's standards.
2. How do you identify what is good and what is bad? How good, or how bad, is something? How do you compare good deeds and bad deeds to keep score? How will you ever know where you stand? Relax – it's just the final outcome of your eternal existence that is dependent on how well you grade yourself.

3. You can always assume that you can do something bad and make up for it by doing something good. What does that do to your heart and soul? How does that affect how you might treat someone on a given day or how you might behave over time?

4. You may be in a situation where you say, "Wait a second! I have been bad for a long time. Oh no! Will I live long enough to be good enough - to do enough good deeds to outweigh the bad?" Or you may be thinking, "I have done some really bad things, and there is no way I can make up for them." The result is the same. You have no hope. You cannot help but think you have blown it.

5. Once you feel you cannot make up for all the bad, you will see no reason for doing good deeds. This is bad for you and for society. You have resigned yourself to hell – if there is one. In this case, you have to hope (and ironically pray!) there is not a hell.

6. Do you have the wisdom to decide what constitutes a good person? Do you really?

7. How can I be certain that I am "good enough" in God's eyes? Can you live in peace not knowing how God views you? This can be a source for constant worry and feelings of hopelessness.

8. A false sense of security can be easily achieved.

9. Do you want subjectivity when the issue is your eternal destiny? Or do you want the promise of an eternal, powerful, loving God? Which offers peace and joy?

So What?

There is one simple, logical truth against which no one can mount an argument, and that is:

Conflicting beliefs cannot all be true. Truth is truth.

Do not fall into the trap of political correctness. With "custom-ordered" religion everyone is viewed as being right, so no person is offended. However, God is offended. There is one true God, and

HE IS WHO HE IS – not how He is defined by different people and religions.

Do not be persuaded by what others' opinions are about God. Opinions are opinions. Go to the right source for knowledge of God. (We will discuss that on Day 4.)

Do not believe sin has no consequences and that occasionally it is all right to disobey His commandments. This will create a separation, not intimacy, between you and God.

Selected Scripture
Psalm 4:2-3   Psalm 50:21   Joshua 24:14-16   Exodus 20:1-4

Prayer
Pray that you will not be tempted to have a low view of God.
Pray that you will not be tempted to define God to fit your needs.

Day 4 – Where Can I Find the True God?

The What

Where can you find a picture of the true God? The answer is The Holy Bible. To know the true God, you must go to the right source for the information. You would not go to a hardware store for milk and eggs; you would go to the supermarket. For information about the one, true God you must go to the right (one true) source, the Holy Bible. Network television, Hollywood, National Geographic, the Discovery Channel, and Time Magazine are not the sources you should depend upon for truth about God. Their motivations can be mixed and based on viewers and subscriptions. Although some philosophers, scholars and scientists can be excellent sources for information, you must be cautious; because their ideas are limited by their knowledge and experiences and are influenced by their personal biases, beliefs and environment. Some may have personal agendas they are trying to push. When we look at the books of other religions, we need to put them under the same kind of scrutiny and forensic tests that the Bible has been under for centuries. Examine these documents and ask these questions:

1. Who wrote these books and how were they assembled?
2. Have they undergone a lot of changes over the years?

3. Do the books contain contradictory statements?
4. Are they supported by history, science and archeology?
5. Are they the writings and insights of one person?

The key is having 100% faith and confidence in the Bible. A great Christian writer, Erwin Lutzer, states that deciding whether to have complete faith in the Bible is "a decision you cannot avoid". (1) He states, "The Bible is either true, or it is a forgery; it is either a good book or an indescribably bad book; it is either the Word of God or the misleading, deceptive words of men." (2)

Let's examine some of the unique reasons you can have faith in the Bible as the inspired Word of God:

✝ The Bible was written over a 1500 year period by forty different God - inspired human authors from many, diverse backgrounds (kings, shepherds, scholars, prophets, a physician, a tax collector, etc.). It was written in three different languages across three continents under many different circumstances (Babylon captivity, prison, desert while traveling, while exiled on an island, etc.). The Bible discusses many diverse topics and theological matters. The Bible presents an incredibly accurate historical account over the same period.

YET

The Bible presents one consistent theme from start to finish: "that is the topic of Christ and the redemption He provided." (3) Lutzer says two words sum up the theme – sin and grace. The messages from the different authors "dovetail with one another, not superficially, but intricately and brilliantly." (4) "The fact that the Bible has unity despite obvious differences in content, style and perspective is a powerful witness to the independence of each author." (5) The Bible claims many times "thus said THE LORD" or that it is inspired by God. The consistency of the Bible lends credible evidence to that point.

✞ The Bible contains extraordinary prophecies, written well in advance of their actual historical occurrence, that have come true with incredible, unfailing accuracy. No other religion has fulfilled prophecies, because only the true God has the knowledge and power to provide accurate prophecies.

✞ Jesus attested to the divine inspiration and truth of the Old Testament Scriptures. See Luke 4:16-21 and Luke 24:44 for examples. Luke 24:44 encompasses all of the Old Testament. Jesus often made reference to Old Testament Scriptures about such men as Adam, Moses, Noah and Jonah.

✞ The Bible was painstakingly and accurately transcribed and preserved. It has not been found to contain errors and it has been unchanged over time. "Jews preserved it as no other manuscript has ever been preserved. With their massora they kept tabs on every letter, syllable, word and paragraph. They had special classes of men within their culture whose sole duty was to preserve and transmit these documents with practically perfect fidelity......" [6]

✞ The Bible is supported by archeology. No archeological discoveries have ever proven the Bible to be in error; however, they often prove it to be accurate and reliable. The renowned Jewish archaeologist, Nelson Glueck states: "It may be stated categorically that no archaeological discovery has ever controverted a Biblical reference." [7]

So What?

Some people pick and choose Bible verses to believe in. They do not have confidence in the Bible as God's Holy Word, and their faith can be weak and can waver when challenged. Their faith will be like waves blown and tossed in the sea. Without the Bible to support them, these people cannot defend their beliefs and can be susceptible to believing anything. They cannot be effective witnesses for Christ.

On the other hand, when you have genuine faith that the Bible is **_the source_** of knowledge and understanding about the true God, you will read and study it more often and with passion. You will come to know the true God, and you can be an effective witness.

Take stock of your faith in the Bible. Read the Bible and put it to the test. Take the step in which Jesus challenged the Jews in John 7:17: **"If anyone chooses to do God's will, he will find out whether my teaching comes from God or whether I speak on my own."** That was a bold statement by Jesus and goes right to the heart of the divine authority of the Gospels.

Selected Scripture

2 Peter 1:20-21	2 Timothy 3:15-17	Matthew 5:17-18
Hebrews 4:12	Isaiah 42:9, 46:9-10	Amos 3:7

Prayer
Thank God for revealing Himself to us through His Holy Word. Ask the Holy Spirit to counsel you so that you will know and understand the truths presented in the Bible.

Day 5 – Knowing God Starts with Seeking God

The What

I love golf and have played it all of my life. One thing I have often heard, and I agree, is that you can really get to know someone by playing golf with them. The person can be a good golfer or a bad golfer – it does not matter. Why is it that you get to know that person? Because when you play enough golf, you will experience many things that are typical in your daily life. You will have good shots and bad shots; you will have good rounds and bad rounds; you will experience good luck and bad luck; you will have opportunities to be honest and to cheat; you will either obey the rules or not; you will be courteous or rude; you will be fun-loving, competitive, hot-tempered, and/or composed; etc. The reason you get to know that person is because each golfer's character is eventually exposed. You get to experience that person for whom he/she is. In golf how you act and how you play the game is very much up to the individual.

The same is true with God. You cannot know God by having someone else tell you about Him, by simply reading about Him, or by talking about Him. You must experience God first-hand; and to do this, you must seek Him – earnestly seek Him. Dr. Charles F. Stanley says, "The expression "seeking God" refers to the desire to know Him – the earnest hungering and thirsting for an intimate relationship with our Creator. It involves an awesome sense of growing oneness with Him, where Jesus Christ is no longer just our distant Savior and Lord but an intimate friend who walks with us moment by moment and day by day." (1)

God is not playing a game of hide-and-seek with us – at least not like a bunch of 10-year olds might play around the neighborhood where the kids put forth an intense effort not to be found. God wants us to seek and to find Him. Maybe this is like a hide-and-seek game that a grandpa might play with his three year old grandson. The grandpa wants to be found and therefore hides where the child will find him. The child only has to make an effort. The child seeks and finds grandpa, feels a sense of accomplishment and learns from the experience. The child is thrilled when he finds his grandpa, sees the smile on his grandpa's face, and receives a loving hug. I imagine God to be much like that based on His desire to be our Father and on the fact that He rejoices over us. The Bible says very clearly **"seek and you will find" (Luke 11:9).**

So What?

Every person is responsible for taking the initiative to seek God. Some will seek; others will not seek. Seeking is not sitting back waiting for God to come to you. The degree to which you seek Him determines how well you will know Him. Take these steps (many of which are clearly identified in Proverbs 2:1-6):

1. Be passionate about knowing God. **"Love the Lord your God with all your heart and with all your soul and <u>with all your mind</u>." (Matthew 22:37)**
2. Pray to God. Talk <u>and</u> listen. Know that He is there hearing every word – knowing your prayers even before you think and speak.
3. Study God's Word. Trust in God's Word.
4. Seek the help of the Holy Spirit, because the Holy Spirit teaches believers about God.
5. Experience God daily in everything. See God in trees and clouds; thank Him when you are enjoying that snack; ask for His help when you have a problem; ask for forgiveness

when you envy someone; just talk with Him when you are troubled. God is there waiting patiently for you.

6. Be still and know that He is God. The great news for you is that if you seek God with your whole heart, you will know Him. This is clearly stated in the Bible. This is a promise of God, and He is faithful. If you had to identify the most important thing in the entire world, Matthew 22:37 probably says it all. God wants us to come to Him with our hearts, so that we have a deep, committed relationship. God wants us to come with our minds, because knowledge about God is good and can lead to that deep relationship. God wants us to come to Him with our souls so that we truly know of Him. He will dwell within us and walk with us daily. Now that is knowledge beyond compare.

Selected Scripture

1 Chronicles 22:19	Jeremiah 29:13	Luke 11:9-10
Proverbs 2:1-6	Psalm 119:2	James 4:8

Prayer

Pray to know God better (which Charles Stanley calls the ultimate goal of prayer). (2)

Seek God in prayer and listen for His response and guidance.

What Are God's Attributes?

Day 6 – The Divine Attributes of God

*A**ttribute**,* as defined by Webster, means an inherent character-istic. In his great book, <u>The Knowledge of the Holy</u>, A. W. Tozer defined attribute as *"whatever God has in any way revealed as being true of Himself."* (1) Now God has told us in Scripture that we, as created human beings, cannot understand everything about Him. However, God has chosen to reveal much about Himself in terms that we can grasp. Perhaps the revelations are enough, in His infinite wisdom, to adequately answer our questions without relinquishing the requirement for faith on our parts. If we could answer all of life's questions intellectually with our minds and without any dependence on our hearts, then we would never strive to truly, deeply know God. God would become nothing more than a text book waiting for us to study and be tested by our mental knowledge of facts about God. God will not let us bring Him down to our level. Study the chart of attributes on the opposite page. Now, we do not pretend to say this is a comprehensive list, but it is a list of most of the recognized and acknowledged attributes.

Examining the attributes of God is a good way for us to under-stand the true nature of God as He has revealed through His Holy Word. As you examine these traits, you must keep in mind several absolute truths that will help you truly know God better:

1. You must not think of these attributes as traits of God, like we would with a person. The traits that constitute a person's

character will change over time and will manifest them-selves differently. They distinguish one person from another. However, with God attributes are not parts that make up God. God is one unitary, Supreme Being. Attributes simply define "how God is". (2)

2. God is 100% of these attributes, 100% of the time. When we say that God is *love,* we are not saying that God is not *jealous* and *just* at the same time. God does "not suspend one to exercise another". (3) In other words, God is love 100% of the time; God is just 100% of the time; God is jealous 100% of the time; God is merciful 100% of the time; etc.

3. These attributes work together in complete harmony and "no contradiction can exist" (4) among these attributes. For example, He is no less good because He is just. His jealousy is not in conflict with His compassion.

4. God's attributes and God's will and purpose cannot be sepa-rated. They are like threads woven together into a fabric. God's will is what it is because of God's attributes, and God's attributes are manifested as His will determines. This is a difficult concept but hopefully will make more sense when we discuss specific attributes.

5. There is one God who exists in three persons: God the Father, God the Son and God the Holy Spirit. All three Persons of the Trinity possess 100% of these attributes, 100% of the time.

6. God is God. We cannot say he is like something or someone else. As good as we can imagine God, He is infinitely better. As wise as we can imagine, He is indeterminately wiser. As loving as we can imagine, He is so much more loving.

Psalm 145: A Praise to God's Attributes and Virtues

Read Psalm 145. Using the chart on the opposite page try to identify and list the many attributes of God portrayed in this one small piece of Scripture. This chapter is a great summary of God's attributes. Now examine this same Scripture and identify and list those things that we will do once we know God. You can compare your list to the list we have provided in Appendix A.

God's Attributes as Defined in God's Word

Perfections of God	Deity of God	Powers of God
Holy	Eternal	Omnipotent
Good	Infinite	Omniscient
Loving	Self-Existent	Omnipresent
Gracious	Self-Sufficient	Sovereign
Merciful	Majestic	Awesome
Faithful	Immutable	Creator/Creative
Patient	Jealous	Wisdom
Compassionate	Divine Transcendence	Sustainer
Just	Glorious	Unlimited
Honest/Trustworthy		

There is one God who exists in three persons: God the Father, God the Son and God the Holy Spirit. All three Persons of the Trinity possess 100% of these attributes, 100% of the time.

Day 7 - The Holy Trinity

The What

Now that we have set the table as to why it is important to truly know the true God, let's begin to study the nature and attributes of God. We will start by examining perhaps the most difficult concept about God – His triune existence, better known as the Trinity. The Trinity is at the heart of Christianity and who God is. The Triune God separates and distinguishes Christianity from other religions, particularly Judaism and Islam.

The Trinity, basically, refers to the God of the Bible - one God that *exists in three persons*: God the Father, God the Son (Jesus Christ), and God the Holy Spirit. Although the word Trinity does not appear in the Bible, all three Persons of the Trinity are mentioned throughout the Bible. Notice at the bottom of the chart in Day 6 where it states that all three Persons of the Trinity possess all of these attributes 100% of the time. The three Persons are equal in power and authority and act in total unity. A. W. Tozer states, "The Persons of the Godhead, being one, have one will." [1]

So why do Christians believe in the Trinity? There are three clear, specific facts that we can glean from Scripture that relate to the Trinity:

There is one, and only one, God.

God exists in three Persons – simultaneously.

1. The Persons work in total unity but at times may perform work separately.
2. The Trinity is in both the Old and New Testaments. Jesus Christ spoke of the Trinity.
3. Let's look at a few examples from our God's own Word.

In Deuteronomy 6:4 the Bible clearly states, **"Hear O Israel: The LORD our God, the LORD is one."** No question there is one God. You should not think that is contradictory to a Triune Godhead. The Hebrew word *echad* is used for "one" whenever God is referred to in the Bible. *Echad* means a compound unity. *Yachid* is the Hebrew word for absolute, singular one. *Yachid* is never used to refer to God. Another, maybe clearer example is that *echad* is used in Genesis 2:24 when the Bible refers to man and woman becoming one (*echad*) flesh. The inspired Word of God uses *echad* for a reason when referring to the one (*echad*) God. As early as Genesis 1:26 we hear: "Then God said: "Let **us** make man in **our** image, in **our** likeness ...""".

The three Persons of the Trinity are often mentioned in the same verses - acting together but with some distinction. In **Luke 3:22** (at baptism of Jesus) we read: **"and the Holy Spirit descended on him (Jesus) in bodily form like a dove. And a voice came from heaven: "You are my Son, whom I (God the Father) love; with you I am well pleased.""** In **Matthew 28:19** Jesus is speaking to His disciples, in what is referred to as The Great Commission, when He says, **"Go therefore and make disciples of all the nations, baptizing them in the name of the Father and the Son and the Holy Spirit"**. In **John 14:16-17** Jesus, immediately prior to His arrest and crucifixion, is speaking to His disciples: **"And I will ask the Father, and He will give you another Counselor to be with you forever – the Spirit of Truth"**. Also in John 14:23: **"Jesus replied, "If anyone loves me, he will obey my teaching. My Father will love him, and _we_ will come to him and make _our_ home with him.""** They abide in us through the Holy Spirit. In fact, Jesus had much to say about the Trinity in chapters 14-17 in the Gospel of John. Read these over and over. They contain so much theology, yet they are so beautifully written. What promises our Savior gives us!

So What?

Have confidence in the Word and believe in the Trinity. There is no doubt that man has limited understanding of the Triune God, as well as why and how He exists as such. However, do not allow your limited understanding to prevent your faith in the Trinity. Again Tozer explains, "The doctrine of the Trinity ... is truth for the heart. The fact that it cannot be satisfactorily explained, instead of being against it, is in its favor. Such a truth had to be revealed; no one could have imagined it." (2)

Selected Scripture

John 8:54-59	Jesus claims Divinity by saying "I AM"; same as God the Father claimed in Exodus 3:14
Matthew 12:28-32	Jesus emphatically points to the Divinity of the Holy Spirit
Romans 8:9-17	The three Persons of the Trinity at work in you; your intimate relationship with God
Colossians 2:9	Deity of Christ
Isaiah 7:14	Immanuel, which means "God is with us"

Prayer

Pray that your understanding and faith of the Trinity will grow.
Pray to God, your Father in heaven; pray for the fullness of the Holy Spirit to dwell within you and for the Holy Spirit to guide you daily; and always pray in Jesus name.

Day 8 – Infinite and Divine Transcendence

The What

God's infinite nature and His divine nature superimpose themselves over all the other attributes. Let's look at an example that includes two of God's other attributes, mercy and love. Two of my favorite verses in the Bible reflect the infinite nature of God's mercy and love, and maybe these verses will help you visualize God's infinitude. I call them my "pointer verses"; because when I read them, I use my finger (or imaginary finger) and point. In Psalm 103:12 David, under the inspiration of the Holy Spirit states: **"as far as the east is from the west, so far has he removed our transgressions from us."** Just point towards the east and the west and imagine two lines going on infinitely into space in opposite directions. Your sins have been removed as far as they can be removed because of God's infinite mercy. In Ephesians 3:17-18 Paul, under the inspiration of the Holy Spirit, writes: **"...And I pray that you, being rooted and established in love, may have the power, together with all the saints, to grasp how wide and long and high and deep is the love of Christ."** Point up, point down, point right, point left, point forwards, and point behind you. Imagine those extending in all directions without limits. There is no container for God's love, because a container would limit His love.

God's infinite nature and His divine transcendence basically mean that He is incomprehensible, incomparable, immeasurable and indescribable. Tozer says that God's "quality of being" (1), His life and existence are exalted infinitely above all He has created. In Exodus 3:13-15 I believe God is expressing this divine transcendence and His infinitude when He tells Moses to tell the Israelites: "I AM WHO I AM". That statement from God probably has more meaning than we can comprehend. Some possible conclusions are:

1. I AM, always have been, and always will be. I transcend time.
2. I AM the source of all things, your Creator. I transcend all things.
3. I AM beyond your understanding. With Me there are no limits, no comparisons, and no measures.
4. I AM your God and there is no other. I am to be exalted above all things.

A. W. Tozer says that God's infinite nature means that He has *no bounds* and is *measureless*. The problem is that we, as created beings, cannot apply our concepts of matter, space and time to God's infinitude. (2) In other words, when you think of God you cannot apply speed, weight, length, amount, numbers, size, quality, degrees, high, low, location, etc. to Him. He is "above all of this, outside of it, beyond it." (3) Clocks, scales, calendars, tape measures, speedometers, etc. are simply not applicable to God. What you have to remember is that God is the Creator, not the created. That one thought makes it easier to conceptualize infinite and divine transcendence.

So What?

God's love, grace, mercy, wisdom, power, knowledge, presence, existence, sovereignty, goodness, majesty, and compassion are without limits. They are without any bounds. Refrain from trying to measure or compare them to anything you can comprehend.

Always keep in mind this wonderful fact. We are created beings, so limits apply to everything about us – except one thing – an infinite eternal future in heaven or hell. God desires that He share His infinite eternity with us.

We simply should not put any limits on God, we should not compare Him to anything in creation. When you do this, you make God less than He is. You start defining God to fit within your limited understanding. Exalt Him above all of His creation. Remember "HE IS WHO HE IS", not who we say He is. Always keep in mind the great "I AM" verses (Exodus 3:13-15 and John 8:58). You will begin to view God as the awesome God He is, and you will know He is worthy of your praise and worship.

When you start to put limits on God's mercy and ability to forgive and start trying to restrict God's love for you, get out your pointer and remember Psalm 103:12 and Ephesians 3:17-18. Oh yea – remember to hold up that pointer and remember who is number one and why He is number one.

Selected Scripture
Psalm 99:5, 103:12, 117:2, 118:1, 147:5   Ephesians 3:14-21

Prayer
Pray Paul's prayer in Ephesians 3:14-21.
Praise God as David did in Psalm 117:2 and 118:1.

Day 9 – Eternal

The What

How would you define eternity? Some men would say it is how long it takes for the wife to get dressed. The ladies might say it is how long it takes the husband to take out the trash. Webster defines eternity as "having infinite duration". Technically that may be correct – but I do not believe that definition does God justice. It is an incomplete definition for the eternal God.

God is eternal. That does not *just* mean He has been around since the beginning of time and will be here until the end of time. It means more than that. You might immediately ask the question: "How can it mean more than from the beginning to the end?" Well, put simply, with God there was no beginning and there will be no end. God created time – just like He did space and matter. Tozer states: "Time marks the beginning of created existence." (1); and, therefore, time is only relevant for created beings. In Revelation 22:13 we have another great "I AM" verse when God the Son tells John: **"I am the Alpha and the Omega, the First and the Last, the Beginning and the End."** This is hard for time-oriented man to comprehend. There was something before time and there will be something after time. There is something outside of time. I hope this isn't giving you a headache!

Time is of no consequence to God. In 2 Peter 3:8, Peter writes: **"But do not forget this one thing, dear friends: With the Lord a**

day is like a thousand years, and a thousand years is like a day."
Peter was making the point that time does not constrain God. God
can be infinitely patient because of His eternal nature. God can also
accomplish an infinite amount instantaneously. God does not have
to do things sequentially because of time. Again Tozer states: "That
God appears at time's beginning is not too difficult to comprehend,
but that He appears at the beginning and end of time *simultaneously*
is not so easy to grasp; yet it is true." (2) Basically, God transcends
time. That is the very reason the prophecies we find in the Bible are
easy for God. That is why other religions, outside of the true God,
do not have fulfilled prophecies.

Years ago there was a TV show called The Time Tunnel. Men
were transported back and forward through time after they acciden-
tally entered the tunnel. I always liked this show because it stirred
the imagination. I imagined points in history that I would like to be
transported so that I could see what and how something occurred.
We cannot jump around in time; but more incredibly, God does not
have to jump around in time. Time is spread out before Him like
one gigantic movie screen. He sees the end from the beginning and
vice versa.

So What?

"Like the sands of an hourglass, so are the days of our lives" is
the lead in to one of television's soap operas. Do you view your life
as an hourglass? One of the biggest problems that people, who do
not know God, have is that time is a consuming beast – consuming
their lives. They see their lives as a limited resource that they must
get the most out of, because it is all they have. They have no hope
for an eternity – much less an eternal life with God in heaven. Tozer
states: "For those out of Christ, time is a devouring beast." (3) Do you
have this problem? I did. It was probably the one greatest obstacle
I had between me and God. I had to try to make the most of every
waking minute. Go for the gusto! "Today we live, for tomorrow we
die!" I was too busy for God. Don't let concern over time be what
keeps you from a relationship with God. Once you realize God has
an unbelievable eternity planned for you, you will become more
patient. You will devote time to God, to His worship, to prayer and

to His Word. You will realize that time is the best reason for having a personal relationship with God. It no longer is the issue it once was.

Knowing that God is eternal should be comforting to you. HE IS WHO HE IS, and has not been caused or impacted by anything else. His eternity and immutability go hand in hand. Because He transcends time, He does not change over time. If He were not eternal, He could not have been the Creator of everything. If He were not eternal, God could not promise us eternity with Him in heaven.

Selected Scripture

Psalm 90:1-2	Psalm 93:2	Ecclesiastes 3:11
Isaiah 40:28	Revelation 22:13	
John 3:15-16; 3:36; 17:1-5, 24		

Prayer

Thank God for His gift of a future eternal life with Him.

Pray for God to help you make the most of your time on earth and that your time here will glorify Him.

Spend quality time now with God so that you can get a small taste of how wonderful it will be to spend an eternity with Him.

Day 10 – Self-Existent and Self-Sufficient

The What

Think for just a minute about the following questions…

1. Where did God come from?
2. Does God need me?

Don't worry if these seem a bit overwhelming or difficult to answer. The brightest minds in the world have struggled with these questions. The problem for many is that the answer depends on faith.

When we say God is self-existent, we mean that nothing caused His existence. He had no origin. Origins and causes relate to created things. And God was not created, but rather He is the Creator. When we say that God is self-sufficient, we mean that God needs nothing to exist. Everything that exists outside of God originates from God and exists because of God. If God were not self-existent and self-sufficient, He would simply not be God. How could God be the Creator of everything, if He is not self-existent? How could God be omnipotent, if He were dependent on something else?

Man often tries to disregard or minimize these attributes of God, because they cannot be explained scientifically or philosophically.

But what it really boils down to is this: do you believe in God and do you believe in Genesis 1:1? A second problem is that man tends to have a very high opinion of ourselves and our importance. When we minimize God's self-existence and self-sufficiency, we define a god that needs us; in other words, He can't get along without us. He needs the angels' help to fight evil; he needs us to defend him; he needs our love or else he will be lonely; he needs his creation to sustain him. Is that a god that is worthy of our worship?

The truth is God exists within Himself, by Himself and for Himself. Each of us should let "Him be the God in our minds that He is in the universe." (1) "That God exists for Himself and man for the glory of God is the emphatic teaching of the Bible." (2) Our belief in God adds nothing to His existence. He exists whether we believe in Him, or not. Our lack of belief does not diminish Him one tiny bit.

So What?

So what importance are these attributes to your daily life? How can you use them like some of the other attributes, such as love, grace, etc.?

When we understand God's self-existence and self-sufficiency, we can begin to better understand the infinite nature of God's love, goodness, mercy and grace. When we say that God does not need us, we are not saying that God does not love us or that we are not important to Him. For some reason, God chose to make us in His image. For some reason, He gave us moral choices and the choice to believe (or not believe) in Him. For some reason, God wants to have a personal relationship with each of us. Other than for His glory, we may not really know why. But we need not know why. The unknown WHY is a matter of faith and trust. God's whole plan of salvation is based on accepting, by faith, His love, goodness, mercy and grace for us.

Personally, I do not find it hard to believe God is self-existent and self-sufficient. I take these on faith. But what is personally hard for me to grasp is why God would love me so much to put up with me. Why would He take on human form and die for my salvation? Why would He tolerate my sins and rebellion? Why? Why? Why?

It is overwhelming to think that while God does not need me, **He desires to:**

- create me in His image
- live / abide within me
- work with me and through me
- have a personal relationship with me
- know me, listen to me
- provide for me with nothing in return
- have a plan that ensures a Way for me to live with Him
- forgive me, over and over and over
- love me, always
- want to spend an eternity with me in His presence

The good thing is that I do not have to fully understand these things. I only have to have faith in what God has promised me when I accept the gift of His Son. The fact that God is sufficient without me and that He does not need me demonstrates His great love for me and His desire to know me personally. That is the ultimate expression of love!

Keep in mind this thought:

God does not need me, it just seems that way because He loves me so much!

Selected Scripture
Psalm 8:3-5   Colossians 1:16-17   John 5:26   Hebrews 2:10

Prayer
Tell God how grateful you are to be special to Him.
Praise and worship Him for the awesome God that He is.
Tell Him that you have faith and trust in Him.
Acknowledge your dependence on Him as Creator, provider and sustainer.

Day 11 – Unchanging and Immutable

The What

R emember in the movie, "Field of Dreams", when the character
played by James Earl Jones was talking about how throughout
the last century of America, even with all the changes, there had
always been one constant – baseball. We could always count on
baseball. Well guess what – I am glad God is not like baseball. Baseball has changed so much – the game, the players, the rules, the fans,
and the game's position in our culture. Salaries have gone crazy;
the game caters to the rich; tickets are expensive; a Coke and a bag
of peanuts cost more than steak dinner; players go on strike; and
football is now the number 1 sport. Hardly a constant! (I still love
baseball.)

Have you ever been reading the Bible and felt like the Scripture
just did not relate to this day and age? Back then the culture was
primitive and agricultural. Today is mechanized and computerized.
Some of the stories are difficult to apply to your circumstances
because of differences in society. Take heart; there is one constant,
one common link between then and now. That is God. God does
not change. God has never changed. God will never change. He is
exactly the same God now to each of us as He was then to the people
in the Bible. How and why doesn't God change? Let's look at a few
reasons provided by J. I. Packer. (1)

1. **"God's life does not change."** (2) Change occurs over time. God transcends time. That is why He is the great "I AM". God also does not get older, wiser, stronger, or better. Arthur Pink states, "He cannot change for the better for He is already perfect; and being perfect, He cannot change for the worse." (3)

2. **"God's character does not change."** (4) God does not love more at one time than another; God is not more or less forgiving now than He was 2,000 years ago; God does not have varying morals; HE IS WHO IS now and forever more.

3. **"God's truth does not change."** (5) God does not change His views or opinions. His promises, His commands, His statements describing good and evil, and all that He has communicated to us is truth now just like it was truth when He inspired its writing 2,000-3,500 years ago. Cultures and societies cannot change God's truths – just like they cannot re-create or change God.

4. **"God's ways do not change."** (6) God still hates sin. God still wants a personal relationship with you. God still works through the lives of His servants. God will act no differently towards us than He did to those in the Bible.

5. **"God's purposes do not change."** (7) His plans are established and never change. His mind does not change. This is because He is wise and omniscient.

6. **"God's Son does not change."** (8) Jesus Christ will always intercede for us; His sacrifice will always be sufficient for our salvation.

So What?

How would you feel about a god that changes? Think about that. A god that changes either gets better or worse, or adapts to changes in his creation. A changing god could not be depended upon or relied upon.

But the God of the Bible is truly THE GOD. You can depend on Him. When He makes a guarantee, you can bank on it. Isn't it comforting to know that your eternal destiny does not depend on a changing god? When He makes a promise, you know He will keep it. A changing god could not and would not be a faithful god.

As a kid or teenager, do you worry about what kind of mood your parents are in before going to them with a request or problem? As far as that goes, husbands, do you pay attention to the mood of your wife before mentioning that you want to play golf this Saturday? Since God is immutable, you need not worry what mood He is in. Tozer writes: "What peace it brings to the Christian's heart to realize that our Heavenly Father never differs from Himself. In coming to Him at any time we need not wonder whether we shall find Him in a receptive mood." (9) Your timing is not an issue with God.

When you plan for retirement, do you ever worry that the government is going to change the tax laws so much that your decisions will turn out completely wrong? What if you live by a set of commands communicated to you by God that He constantly changes so that you do not have a clear picture of right and wrong? With God, you know what His commands are, and you know that they will be in effect now and forever. This is because God's holiness is perfect and does not change.

Ever been traveling and thought you knew the way but got lost because the roads had changed so much? If God is not immutable, would you really have confidence in your salvation? Take comfort in the fact that what Jesus said in John 14:4 is still truth: **"You know the way to the place where I am going."**

Selected Scripture
Psalm 102:26-27; 119:89, 151-152   Malachi 3:6   James 1:17
Isaiah 40:6-8

Prayer
Thank God for being the same yesterday, today and tomorrow.
Thank God for being dependable in all of His ways and how He acts towards you.
Pray that you <u>will change</u> to be more Christ-like through the work of the Holy Spirit in you.

Day 12 – Glorious and Majestic

The What

Majestic! Glorious! Greatness! Magnificence! Grand! Incomparable!

We should always think of God in these terms. But that is easy to do when we flood our minds with the thought of God's attributes and with His creation. What an awesome God! Soak in God's majesty; revel in it; dwell on it. Be still and know that He is God! (from Psalm 46:10) When you do grasp His majesty, you will have no problem humbling yourself before Him, praising Him, and worshipping Him. That is why focusing on God's majesty is so important!

Knowing and understanding God is a key to growing in our personal relationship with Him. But we must be careful not to confuse God's personal nature with God being a person. This will create a low view of God – a small God. God has none of the weaknesses or limitations of man. He is personal – but never let this take away from His majesty.

In Isaiah chapter 40:12-31, we get a clear picture of how awesome God's majesty really is. With what can we compare God?

Verse 12	He is greater than His creation.
Verse 13	Who can understand God's mind? Who can give Him guidance?
Verse 14	Who can teach God? Who can show God wisdom?
Verses 15-17	He is greater than any nation. Nations are so little they do not even weigh on His scales. Even rich Lebanon's trees and animals are not sufficient for adequate sacrifice for worshipping the majestic, almighty God. Nations cannot compare – they are as nothing.
Verses 18-20	No image or idol is worthy of God. No matter if made from gold.
Verses 21-22	God is before creation. God is over and above this world.
Verses 23-25	God is greater than any ruler – ever. They are nothing. They come and they go. God's sovereignty controls this world.
Verse 26	God created and is above all in the heavens (space).
Verse 27	Why do we think we are too small or insignificant for God? He knows everything about us and He easily can attend to all problems without disregarding any.
Verses 28-30	He is eternal. He is the Creator. He never tires or grows weary. His energy is infinite. Even men in the prime grow tired and weary. But God sustains all.
Verse 31	God can make "you soar like an eagle" if you put your hope in Him. God can do whatever He chooses.

To me, verse 26 demonstrates God's majesty and awesomeness as well as any verse. It hits on perhaps the most majestic of all of God's creations – a vast, finely tuned universe with all the stars, moons, planets, galaxies, and systems. I love this verse! Millions of galaxies! Trillions upon trillions of stars! Billions of light years of space! And earth is in just the right galaxy, in just the right solar system, in just the perfect location and orbit, with just the right composition, etc. etc. etc. Packer states, "Our minds reel; our imaginations cannot grasp it; when we try to conceive of unfathomable depths of outer space, we are left mentally numb and dizzy." (1) But even in all of this majesty we see the personal nature of God when the Bible tells us that He calls the stars out by name. Now that is a glorious and majestic God who takes great joy and pleasure in His creation! Just another reason to worship His majesty!

So What?

J. I. Packer believes that we should respond to God's majesty in three ways. First, do not have *"wrong thoughts about God"*. (2) Don't insult God by bringing Him down to your level. Dr. Charles Stanley says that God's majesty is the very reason He hates idolatry and why it makes Him angry. (3) It is the second of the Ten Commandments. After giving Moses the commandment, God provides the reason for the commandment - His jealousy. When we insult God and His majesty we will suffer the consequences. On the flip side, we will experience the fullness of life when we have great thoughts about God. Think of God's majesty by pulling together all of God's attributes. Do not limit in your mind what He can do. Do not limit His ability to deliver on His promises. See Isaiah 40:25.

Second, do not have *"wrong thoughts about ourselves"*. (4) As insignificant as you may seem in this vast creation, God has promised that you are special and will receive His individual attention – even more so than the trillions of stars. Do not have a pessimistic faith wondering if God hears you, cares about you, or has forgotten you. This dishonors God's majesty. See Isaiah 40:27.

Third, do not be *"slow to believe in God's majesty"*. (5) If you find yourself in this frame of mind, make a conscious effort, through prayer and meditation and reading God's Word, to acknowledge and believe in His majesty.

Selected Scripture
Isaiah 40:12-31   Psalm 93

If time permits you, Psalm 139 and chapters 36-41 in Job depict God's majesty.

Prayer
Praise God for His majesty.

Thank God that you are special to Him – even though you might appear insignificant within the vastness of His creation.

Day 13 – Omniscient and Wise

The What

W hen we say that God is omniscient we mean that He is all-knowing, or knows everything. Another way of saying this is that there is nothing God does not know. His knowledge is perfect and complete. Since God knows everything, He is never learning or surprised or befuddled. God does not have to perform research to discover scientific facts since He created everything and knows how everything functions. God is omnipresent, so nothing is hidden from Him. God transcends time, so He does not have to wait to see what is going to happen. The Bible tells us that God knows our thoughts and motives; and as Luke 16:15 says, **"God knows your hearts"**.

Does it bother you that God knows everything about you – everything you do, say and think? God knows what is in each of our hearts, not just our external actions and conduct. For example, Jesus spoke against the sin of being angry or of hating another person, not just against physical harm or murder. Evil acts flow out of evil thoughts. The omniscience of God means that He knows the evil within your heart and mind as well as all of your evil actions! You cannot do anything in secret, and you cannot lie to cover up your deeds. Ah – but the good news! A saved person can take comfort in Romans 5:8. Even though God knows your sins, He sent Jesus Christ into the world to die as a payment for all of them.

The mind-boggling aspect of this salvation through Jesus Christ is that God not only forgives your sins, but He chooses to forget them. God chooses to limit Himself, His omniscience, by completely forgetting your sins when you trust in His plan of salvation and redemption. That is the *power* of Jesus' resurrection. God allows your trust and faith in Him to actually impose a limitation on Him! Isaiah 43:25 tells us that God will choose, for His own sake (will), to not remember our sins. Think about the old-fashioned blackboard that we used to have in school. Now imagine all of your sins are listed on the board. (It would have to be a big blackboard for my list!) God does not just cross through each sin; God does not just erase every sin; He washes the board clean so that you cannot tell that anything was written there. There is not even a hint of chalk dust!

Now let's examine God's perfect wisdom. God's perfect wisdom means that all of His plans, decisions and acts are the perfect means to perfect ends. His perfect wisdom coincides with His many other attributes: His omniscience, holiness, goodness, sovereignty, omnipotence, and His ability to see everything "from the end to the beginning." (1) The question is: do we have faith that God can bring all of His powers together and provide perfect solutions? Tozer states that "All God's acts are done in perfect wisdom, first for His own glory, and then for the highest good of the greatest number for the longest time. And all His acts are as pure as they are wise, and as good as they are wise and pure. Not only could His acts not be better done: a better way to do them could not be imagined." (2) That's a mouthful, but worth reading again.

Accept the fact that you will never have the understanding of God's wisdom. This is where your faith and belief in God step in and your knowledge, understanding and wisdom take a backseat. In John 20:20 Jesus told Thomas: **"blessed are they that have not seen, and yet have believed."** Another way of thinking about this verse is: "blessed are all who believe without understanding everything." You can ask a million "why" questions for which you will never have the answers. Why does God allow evil? Why do bad things happen to good people? Why is there a hell? Why is my child suffering? But here is the key point. In true faith you must accept that God's infinite wisdom (along with His love, goodness, etc.) *"will bring about the best possible results, by the best possible means, for the most people, for the longest possible time."* (3) With your limited insight and wisdom you may not know or understand why it is the best, but in faith you accept God's wisdom as perfect.

So What?

So how can you use your faith in God's omniscience and wisdom on a practical, daily basis? One way is to have peace when faced with life's difficult problems. You can take comfort knowing God understands your problems. Believe that God's wisdom is infinite and that He applies it for "the best possible results in your life by the best possible means." (4) Do not expect to understand everything, but don't stop seeking God's counsel.

Know that having faith in God and God's wisdom does not mean that you will be given special revelations about what is to occur or why they occur. You may never be able to explain most of what happens in this world – plain and simple. He has said that you will have trials while on earth. Sometimes the bad will triumph over the good. Things will seem to occur haphazardly. Death, disease, injuries, financial problems, disasters, etc. will sometimes happen to good people while the seemingly bad go on prospering. Sometimes it will look like God is not in control – but you must keep in mind you have a very limited view and insight. J. I. Packer wrote: "For the truth is that God in his wisdom, to make and keep us humble and to teach us to walk by faith, has hidden from us almost everything that we should like to know about the providential purposes which he is working out in the churches and in our own lives." (5)

Chip Ingram says that you need to live wisely, which means "living in accordance with God's Word." (6) Spend time in God's Word and your wisdom will grow. Ingram writes that he hates to read instruction manuals. Me, too. "But when it comes to life... there's just too much at stake not to pay attention to God's instruction manual." (7)

<u>Selected Scripture</u>
Psalm 103:12; 119:97-101; 139:1-6   Isaiah 43:25   Luke 16:15
Romans 11:33-36

<u>Prayer</u>
Start praying today for guidance and wisdom in every situation and opportunity that life presents to you.

Ask God to clarify His will for you.

Ask for strength when you don't understand why something is happening.

Praise God for His wisdom and acknowledge that you desire His will to be done.

Day 14 – Omnipotent and Omnipresence

The What

The word omnipotent means "all power". The word omnipresent means "all present". These two attributes describe God and only God. He is all powerful and He is present everywhere. That's hard for our finite minds to comprehend, but remember, we are talking about an INFINITE God.

Tozer says this about God's omnipotence: "Since He has at His command all the power in the universe, the Lord God omnipotent can do anything as easily as anything else. All His acts are done without effort. He expends no energy that must be replenished. His self-sufficiency makes it unnecessary for Him to look outside of Himself for a renewal of strength. All the power required to do all that He wills to do lies in undiminished fullness in His own infinite being." (1) Many times the Bible uses the word almighty for God's infinite, absolute power.

God's omnipotence means He has power over His entire creation. This may seem obvious, but some people have a hard time coming to terms with it. Many people doubt some of the miracles in the Bible because the miracles violate the "laws of nature". We should not limit God's power to constraints we call "laws of nature". These "laws" are natural phenomena created by God to provide order and predictability within His creation. God's power easily allows Him to override any of these forces of His creation, thereby performing what we think of as miracles – but to Him are just further exercises of His power.

Omnipresence means that God is everywhere simultaneously, always close to everything. God can be omnipresent because God is spirit. When you think of God do you picture Him sitting on a throne in Heaven and confined there – and maybe by some special power just being able to "see" what is happening in the world? The Bible does depict God as residing in heaven but it also states that God is everywhere. God is not a physical being. His spirit exists in and around all created things.

Could God be omniscient or omnipotent without being omnipresent? If He were not omnipresent, there would be things going on in which He would not be aware. He could not exercise His power everywhere without His presence being everywhere or without His knowing everything. He might be powerful – but He would not be ALL powerful or ALL mighty. God's attributes work together in complete harmony and in support of each other – 100% of His attributes, 100% of the time. HE IS WHO IS.

So What?

So how can you use your knowledge of God's omnipotence and omnipresence in your daily life? As a Christian, you should find comfort in God's almighty power, which ensures you that He can do what He has promised. These are not empty promises which He cannot deliver. Take heart in the fact that He will use that power to shield you forever. See 1 Peter 1:3-5.

God's infinite power can be a source of power within you. God does not give away any of His power to you but will willingly share it with you. How does He share His power?

Through your prayers   James 5:16
Through His Word   Romans 1:16
Through His Holy Spirit   Ephesians 1:17-19

Through Jesus	Ephesians 3:14-21
	Colossians 1:11
	Philippians 4:13
Through His resurrection	Philippians 3:10

Let the knowledge that you are never alone calm the troubled sea of your life and speak peace to your soul. (2) Know that God is immediately accessible to you through Jesus Christ. Jesus promised he would be with you always to the very end.

Experience the presence and fullness of the Holy Spirit within you. Your courage, confidence and understanding will increase. You will experience the fruit of the Spirit – joy, love, peace, patience, kindness, goodness, faithfulness and self-control.

Selected Scripture
See above list which identifies how God shares His power with us.
Psalm 66:1-7; 139:7-10   Job 42:2   Matthew 28:20
1 Peter 1:3-5

Prayer
Pray for a personalization of God's power in your prayers.
Ask for Him to make known His presence during you prayers.
Ask to experience His power through the work of the Word and the Holy Spirit.
Pray to feel His presence at work in your life.

Day 15 – Faithful, Honest and Trustworthy

The What

Think back to the old westerns that used to be in the theatres and on television. I loved to sit in front of the old black and white TV on Saturday mornings and watch the westerns. I can remember all of the cowboy heroes and their horses. My favorites were the Lone Ranger and his horse Silver and Roy Rogers and his horse Trigger. The vivid image of the Lone Ranger yelling "hi-ho Silver" as the stallion rocked back on its hind legs, standing tall and off they would go to save somebody from the bad guys still fills my mind. Then there was Roy Rogers and Trigger flying down the dirt trail with the horse's mane flying in the breeze hurrying to rescue someone. You could always depend on the heroes, and they could always depend on their horses. Maybe that is why Revelation 19:11 creates such a vivid image in my mind:

> **"I saw heaven standing open and there before me was a white horse, whose rider is called Faithful and True."**

This is Jesus Christ as He appears at His second coming. Does that not send chills up your back!!! Of all of God's attributes and possible titles, He chose to emphasize *Faithful and True* for Christ at the time He rescues the world from evil and brings justice to the world. God wants you to know His promises (in this case being Jesus' return, judgment, etc.) are truth and that He will be faithful to them. I have to wonder what that white horse's name will be. Maybe something like Rock of Ages or Satan's Demise! What do you think?

God's faithfulness means that we can depend on Him. Our hope in Christ is not wishful thinking but is, instead, a <u>confident expectation</u> of what is to come. Know that God is honest all the time. God does not lie. God cannot lie – else He would not be a Holy God. When God tells us something in His Word, we know it is the truth. Because God is faithful, we also know that we can depend on God to fulfill all of His promises that He has spoken. When God says something, He is committed to it. He does not change His mind because He is perfect in His wisdom and unchanging in His character. God is omnipotent so He is able to deliver on His promises. He is, therefore, worthy of our trust all the time. See how God's attributes work together and complement each other!

David was a man after Gods' heart, because he loved and trusted God. Just look at the Book of Psalm and see how many times David said trust in the LORD. When David referred to God as his rock, he was praising God's unchanging nature and on the fact that he could trust Him without reservation. Here are a few examples:

Psalm 9:10	"Those who know your name will trust in you, for you, LORD have never forsaken those who seek you."
Psalm 18:2	"The LORD is my rock, my fortress and my deliverer, my God is my rock, in whom I can take refuge."
Psalm 19:7	"The law of the LORD is perfect, reviving the soul. The statutes of the LORD are trustworthy…"
Psalm 25:1-2	"To you, O LORD, I lift up my soul; in you I trust O my God."
Psalm 33:4	"For the Word of the LORD is right and true; he is faithful in all he does."

| Psalm 37:4 | "Commit your way to the LORD; trust in him and he will do this..." |
| Psalm 145:13 | "The LORD is faithful to all His promises..." |

So What?

Let's focus on one of God's foundational promises (maybe the greatest) in the Bible. God's Word promises you in 1 John 1:9 that God will forgive your sins – all of your sins. **"If we confess our sins, he is *faithful* and just and will forgive us *all* our sins and purify us from *all* unrighteousness."** This is a promise you can take to the bank. When God says everyone, all, forever, etc., He means what He says. He does not mean most or a long time or a vast majority. He means all – without exception. You may be thinking "I've done some really bad things" or "I've done way too many bad things" or "I've done so many bad things for such a long time" there is no way even God can forgive me. Do not think that because you cannot forgive yourself that God cannot forgive you. I like what Chip Ingram says: "When Jesus died on the cross, a transaction occurred. He covered your sin once and for all. The issue is whether you will accept that God's solution for sin is true in your case. If God is faithful and just, then Christ's blood atoned for your sin, and forgiveness is available to you. It's not about you forgiving you; it's about you accepting what God has done. Not to do so underestimates the blood that Christ shed for you." (1) Do not make God out to be dishonest, unfaithful or impotent to do what He has promised. He promised to forgive and forget your sins.

Let's quickly look at other foundational promises you can take to the bank because of God's honesty, faithfulness and trustworthiness.

- You can bank on future prophecies about the end times. The inerrant accuracies and 100% fulfillment of Biblical prophecies to-date are evidence of His faithfulness.
- Know that Jesus Christ will return to reign on earth. God promised a Messiah in the form of a sacrificial lamb, and He

delivered. He promises that Jesus will return a second time as a roaring lion that will conquer evil and judge mankind.

- Know that faith in God and Jesus Christ as your Lord and Savior will result in the gift of your eternal life in heaven. Jesus plainly stated this promise in John 14:1-4. Trust in God and in His faithfulness and you will have hope – that confident expectation – that your loving Father will deliver on His promise of a glorious eternity in heaven for you – His child. You are a co-heir with Christ!
- Do not doubt that there will be eternal punishment in hell for rejection of God.
- Be 100% assured that God loves you.
- Have confidence in the power of the Holy Spirit. Once you have been saved, Jesus promises that you will never be lost – never.
- Trust in the power of prayer and that God hears your prayers.
- Have total confidence in God's Word as truth.

Have faith in God's faithfulness!

Selected Scripture
Deuteronomy 7:9   Numbers 23:19   Psalm 108:4
Isaiah 11:5, 25:1   Titus 1:2   1 Corinthians 1:9
Hebrews 6:16-20, 10:19-23
1 Thessalonians 5:23-24   2 Thessalonians 3:3

Prayer
Ask God to strengthen you when doubts creep into your thoughts. Praise God for all of His foundational promises that you can take to the bank.

Day 16 – Patient

The What

I am so grateful for the patience of God. God could limit His goodness, love, mercy and grace to those who come to know Him early in their lives and go on to live righteous lives. However, God's patience, driven by His love and goodness for us, means that He withholds His wrath and judgment from those who sin over a period of time. (1) I am still amazed at how God put up with my behavior for so long. Why did He not just wipe me out and be done with me? Anyone who has ignored God or rebelled against God for any part of their lives should be incredibly grateful for God's patience. It means that as long as you live, you can still be saved, become a child of God, and be under God's grace. That is the very reason God says He is so patient with man. He desires to see us saved and that none would be lost.

As we look at God's attributes many may think that there is a contradiction in God's nature. Can God be good, merciful, gracious and loving and also be just (judging), jealous and wrathful? Yes – and one reason is because of His patience. God wants the best for us, and He patiently withholds His judgment and wrath to give us every opportunity to come to Him. So why is God patient with us? He is patient not because of who we are, but because of who He is. We are not good and deserving of His patience. We are all sinners "in dirty rags" before the holiness of God. God is patient because of who He is – a good and loving and merciful and gracious God.

One of the toughest questions that you might ask is: "does God's patience have a limit?" In Exodus 32, God's patience appears to have been fairly brief for the 3,000 that were slain at Mt. Sinai after they worshipped the golden calf. The Bible does not say if they were the only ones who worshipped or if they led the worship or if they worshipped the calf more intensely. Again in Acts 5, it appears that God's patience quickly ran out for Ananias and Sapphira when they lied to God. His wrath fell on them quickly. On the other hand, God appears to have been extremely patient with the Jewish nation after Solomon's reign as they continuously rebelled against God over hundreds of years. God was very patient with David, Peter, and Paul.

So how do we come to terms with these perceived contradictions in God's patience? We need to keep in mind two key truths. First, you have been given the freedom to make choices every day, and there are consequences to those choices. You cannot know these consequences, and you cannot choose these consequences. Second, God's attributes not only work in complete harmony with each other, they operate in conjunction with His overall will and purpose. God has an overall purpose for His creation and for each of us. Again we must trust God and have faith in His wisdom, goodness, and purpose even though we cannot understand it completely.

So What?

If you have not accepted Christ and are continuing to live in sin, be grateful that you are alive and able to read this. God has been patient with you. Eventually you will die (and you know not when), or you will miss the rapture. Right now, even after years of sinning many sins, it is not too late to avoid God's wrath. Tomorrow – who knows – it may be too late.

God's patience is continuously at work in your life. When you sin, the Holy Spirit convicts you of your sin. In other words, the Holy Spirit reveals to you that what you are doing is sin. God also disciplines you, sometimes immediately and sometimes later, so that you realize there are consequences to sin. So God:

convicts – convicts – convicts – convicts
and
disciplines – disciplines – disciplines – disciplines

This is God patiently at work giving you many opportunities to come to Him.

But God's patience is not a reason to assume you can keep putting off making a decision to live in Christ. We have no assurance or guarantee of tomorrow. We must respond to God's patience today as we have opportunity.

Selected Scripture
1 Peter 3:20   2 Peter 3:8-9, 15   Romans 2:4   Psalm 103:8

Prayer
Praise God for His goodness and love that are revealed in His patience. If you are saved, thank God for being alive long enough for the Holy Spirit to draw you to Christ.

If you are caught up in continuous sin, ask for the Holy Spirit to help you overcome the sin that has you captive.

Pray that God will be patient with our country, which has rejected God as an important part in our country's government.

Day 17 – Good and Compassionate

The What

A. W. Tozer states: "The goodness of God is that which disposes Him to be kind, cordial, benevolent, and full of good will toward men." (1) Think about what that means. If the supreme being of the universe was not 100% good, 100% of the time, then you would never know what to expect. We might find that "His good pleasure" had nothing to do with our good pleasure. However, God's goodness is His desire to want what is best for you and me, and that includes a full life here on earth and eternity with Him in heaven. God's goodness is the reason we can trust Him. There are so many ways we can discuss God's goodness, but let's just look at God's goodness in a couple of simple ways.

I love chocolate! Chocolate ice cream - I love to savor chocolate ice cream. Stir it around in the bowl until it is soft and creamy and then let it slide down the palate. Or one of my favorites, a big bowl of chocolate ice cream with bananas, pecans and pancake syrup. A Hershey's chocolate candy bar slowly melting and dissolving in my mouth gives me a glimpse of what heaven will be like. My wife goes to the trouble of special ordering a chocolate fudge sauce from Michigan that goes great over ice cream and brownies. Oh boy - brownies and milk just go so good together. My wife makes a homemade chocolate "Mounds" candy with coconut and pecans that is dangerous, because I cannot stop eating them. Then there is my

Mom's homemade chocolate pudding (that my wife also makes). I can't describe this one. Just know that for me it is a true religious experience – because I can thank God for moments like that. God's goodness means He takes pleasure in my pleasure. When it comes to chocolate, I am so happy and grateful that I can bring Him so much pleasure.

I can't even begin to imagine how evolutionists explain something like chocolate. To me, chocolate is evidence of God's creativity, omniscience and goodness. He must have thought, "I will make this plant that will produce cocoa beans, and man will learn to cultivate and harvest them. He will creatively use these beans to produce this substance he will call chocolate, and then he will use this chocolate to bring pleasure to himself." I can't think of another reason for chocolate, other than God's pure, good disposition to man, because man could live without it. I could exist, but I would miss out on one of life's simple pleasures that God has given me. Thank you, Lord; thank you; thank you; thank you.

Goodness also needs to be looked at from another angle. The Bible says that fearing God is the beginning of wisdom and the Bible plainly states that we are to fear the Lord God. But I like what Tozer says in regards to this: "The greatness of God rouses fear within us, but His goodness encourages us not to be afraid of Him. To fear and not be afraid – that is the paradox of faith." (2) To me that is a very good understanding of God. Once you truly know God you understand His holiness and will have reverent fear (and awe) of Him; but you will also understand God's goodness and compassion and not be afraid of the Lord. God tells us He is good, and on that I can rest assured.

So What?

It's so easy to think about God's magnificent creation in the big picture. But if you don't take the time to look at all the little things that personally impact you, you will miss the true wonders of God's goodness to you as an individual. Take the time today to have a "chocolate moment" and thank God for His little, personal creations that make your life enjoyable. Your understanding of God's true love for you will grow, and so will your love for Him.

Take comfort in the fact that you can trust your God to want what is best for you. Tozer states, "The goodness of God is the drive behind all of the blessings He daily bestows upon us." (3)

When bad things happen, do not equate this with the absence of God's goodness. God is good all of the time. The Bible tells you that you will experience troubles on earth. You will be troubled, sad and broken-hearted at times. Reflecting on God's goodness and love will help you weather these storms. God's goodness assures you that He has compassion for you.

Above all, keep your eyes on the promise that originates from God's love and goodness, the promise of a trouble-free, magnificent eternity that awaits you when you put your faith in Jesus Christ. One day when you depart from this earth, know that you will stand before a holy God – but a God that is good and loving and faithful.

Selected Scripture

Psalm 84:11	James 1:16-18	Romans 8:31-32
Ephesians 3:12	Exodus 34:5-6	Psalm 106:1, 107:1
John 10:11-15		

Prayer

Thank the Lord for His goodness towards you.

Thank Him for the many small things that you enjoy every day.

Praise Him for having compassion on you, a sinner, and for the hope that we have in eternal life with Him.

Day 18 – Just

The What

Scenario #1:

"Order in the court! Order in the court! All rise for Judge…." If you are ***not saved***, I don't think you will hear those words when you face God at the Great White Throne Judgment. There will be no lawyer there to defend you, no jury to try to convince. You have rejected your only advocate, Jesus, and so you will appear before Almighty God defenseless. There will be no pleading "nolo contendere" in hopes of getting a light sentence. God will not be bargaining with you over your punishment. The Book of Deeds will be opened and your life will be laid wide open as the evidence of your rejection of God. If you are not saved, I think that as soon as you appear before God you will be doing the opposite of rising. You will be doing – probably out of holy terror - what the Bible states in Philippians 2:10 and Isaiah 45:23: ""As surely as I live", says the Lord, "every knee will bow before me; every tongue will confess to God."" You will realize the futility of your the arguments of how good a person you were on earth when you face the holy God with all of your thoughts, motives and actions made evident. You will realize it is too late to accept the gift of grace, because the gift has been permanently taken back since you rejected it all through your life. That sinking feeling of regret will enter your mind and then suddenly you realize it will be with you for eternity. The gavel will come down and you will be forever swept into eternal damnation.

Scenario #2:

You are swept into heaven before the Almighty God. The first words you hear might be: "(*your name*), welcome to heaven. I have been waiting for you to be here with Me. I have prepared a place especially for you, and you will be dining with Me tonight." Beautiful sounds; warm, loving embraces; spectacular surroundings; the glory of God completely filling every thing and every one; wondrous sights; feelings of unbelievable greatness;... Then you realize that only by the grace of God you will spend eternity in heaven with brothers and sisters in Christ in the presence of God. You too, will be bowing before God – but out of love, thankfulness, adoration, praise and worship.

Webster defines justice as the assignment of merited rewards or punishment. To be just means to treat fairly and without partiality. In other words, when you are treated justly – you get what you deserve. So what do you think – which scenario above is just? The answer is both. In Scenario #1, you got what you deserved for your sin and rejection of God. You rejected and defied God, rejected His gift of salvation, rejected His grace and mercy and love, refused to trust God, and selfishly focused on yourself. God was unimportant or non-existent. You stand before God unholy. Therefore, God's punishment is just. In Scenario #2 you do not get what you deserve when compared to the holy, perfect standard of God. Only by God's love, mercy and grace do you receive eternal life in heaven. However, in God's eyes, Jesus has paid the price for your sin so that you can stand before God holy and sin free. God simply does not see or remember your sins and guilt, so the reward is just to God.

Know that God cares about the distinction between right and wrong. Moral indifference would be an imperfection; God would not be righteous. J. I. Packer states: "The final proof that God is a perfect moral Being, not indifferent to questions of right and wrong, is the fact that he has committed himself to judge the world." [1]

So What?

Make no mistake - God is just and will render to you what you deserve. God's Word talks much about His judgment, and you need to understand and apply this knowledge to the way you live your life.

1. Without salvation through Jesus Christ, your name will not be in the Book of Life; you will be found guilty; and you will be eternally punished. Do not let what Tozer says apply to you: "The vague and tenuous hope that God is too kind to punish the ungodly has become a deadly opiate for the consciences of millions. It hushes their fears and allows them to practice all pleasant forms of iniquity while death draws nearer and the command to repent goes unregarded." (2) **(Born once, die twice! Born twice, die once!)**

2. Repenting of sins is essential. Trust in God to forgive. "If we confess our sins, he is *faithful* and *just* and will forgive us our sins and purify us from *all* unrighteousness." (1 John 1:9)

3. Regardless of whether you are saved, God will judge you by the deeds you have done on earth. There will be degrees of reward for the saved. Live your life in service to the Lord, with goodness and righteousness in your heart, and you will be rewarded accordingly. Keep in mind deeds include not only things you did, but also things you should have done – but didn't. (such as feeding the hungry)

4. Your judgment will depend on the availability of God's Word to you, how you received the Word, and your ability to know and understand God's Word. I cannot imagine many valid excuses most of us in America could have for not knowing and not applying God's Word. Much will be expected of you. I think God's justice will take into account age, mental capacity, physical disabilities, limitations imposed by poverty and family life; but for the most part, an ordinary American has ready access to churches, Bibles and the truth. Your judgment and rewards will depend on your willingness

to receive God and have the Holy Spirit work through you as well as the goodness that flows from your heart.

Selected Scripture (read as many as time allows)

Romans 2:6-11	2 Corinthians 5:10	Matthew 16:27
Luke 12:47-48	John 3:18-19, 5:22-30	1 Corinthians 3:11-15
Acts 17:31	Ecclesiastes 12:14	Revelation 20:11-13

Prayer

Pray to God that He will move you to discover and use your spiritual gifts to serve Him.

Praise God for His justice and thank Him for His mercy and grace.

Day 19 – Merciful and Gracious

The What

When I was about 8 years old, my older brother and I got into a fight. Nothing serious, but we were going at it (mainly wrestling) in the den. Mom and Dad were at work. We moved the wrestling match up on the couch. The fight ended when I pushed him and he went through the picture window behind the couch. Fortunately the curtain kept him from getting hurt by the broken glass. My brother and I went from being ferocious fighters to cowards – wondering how bad the whipping was going to be. Right before Mom and Dad came home we both put on two pairs of blue jeans and stuffed some magazines in the seat and legs of the jeans. To our surprise, our parents did not punish us. Instead of anger, they showed my brother and me *mercy*. Perhaps they were both so happy that my brother did not get hurt that they couldn't whip us, but that was because they loved us so much. For some unknown reason, they didn't even make us pay for it out of our allowance. Now I realize how *gracious* they were to both of us. Not only did we not get the just punishment we probably deserved (at least what we thought we were going to get), but we also got to keep our allowance – an undeserved benefit.

The word "gospel" means good news. God's mercy and grace are at the very heart and core of this good news. The single most important truth that every Christian should know and believe has to do with God's mercy and grace. As a Christian you should - strike that - _**must**_ have 100% confidence in God's mercy and grace. It is one thing to believe God exists; but until you grasp God's mercy and grace, you will never truly know God. You will never understand God's plan of salvation, nor will you look at God as your Father. The ultimate expression of God's love for you is seen in His mercy and grace. The ultimate expression of your faith in God is your faith in His grace and mercy. Once you have this faith, you know that God truly loves you, forgives you, and has eternal treasures planned for you. Basically, you know the truth and the truth sets you free.

When we talk about God's mercy and grace, what do we really mean? To me, mercy and grace go hand-in-hand. They flow from and express God's love to us who have faith in Him and in Jesus Christ as our Lord and Savior. *Mercy* is the attribute of His "divine nature which disposes God to be actively compassionate". (1) As a child of God, His mercy means that He will not punish you for your sins. This translates to the forgiveness of your sins. "*Grace* is the good pleasure of God that inclines Him to bestow benefits upon the undeserving." (2) In other words, God not only forgives your sins, He remembers them no more – to the point of giving you eternal blessings and rewards in heaven. This is often referred to as God's "unmerited favor" towards us.

God's grace and mercy are infinite and available to us at all times. Do not think of these gifts as relevant only at the moment of salvation or at the time you enter heaven. Lean on and stand in God's grace every day and in every situation. "Believe that God's mercy is boundless, free and, through Jesus Christ our Lord, available to us now in our present situation." (3) This is what leads to the peace and confidence that Paul and John spoke of that comes with the understanding of God's mercy and grace.

The problem most of us have – and I am guilty of this one – is that we do not readily accept the fact that God has completely forgiven us. We either think that: (1) we have committed too many sins; (2) we have repeated the same sin so many times; or (3) the sins we have committed are just too bad or evil to be forgiven. No matter how much we ask for forgiveness we cannot feel like we are forgiven. R.C. Sproul says that we are falling for the lies of Satan, because his primary mission is to accuse Christians of their sin, attempting to make them feel unforgiven and unworthy, and thereby separating them from God. We trust our feelings of guilt and unworthiness rather than the promises of God. Look at the chart below. This summarizes some of the basic truths about God's mercy and grace. (4)

Real Sin	All have sinned	1 John 1:8, 10
		Romans 3:23
↓		
Real Guilt	Holy Spirit convicts us	John 16:8
↓		
Real Repentance	True sorrow in the heart	2 Cor 7:10
↓		
Real Forgiveness	God will forgive	1 John 1:9

We have all sinned and will probably continue to sin as long as we live. However, if you truly feel sorrow and regret for your sins, confess them and repent, and ask for forgiveness, God will forgive your sins. His mercy and grace are a free gift. You can do nothing to earn this forgiveness. Think of it as a debt you cannot pay and without God's mercy and grace you are doomed to spiritual bankruptcy.

So What?

Know that, not just you, but everybody sins. In 1 John 1:8 and 10, John tells us that we are liars if we claim to be pure and without sin and that we make God out to be a liar. So do not feel like you are the Lone Ranger of sinners.

Trust the objective truth of the Scriptures regarding God's mercy and grace - rather than your subjective feelings, which make you feel unforgiven. God has promised you that He will forgive your sins. You could use similar wording to 1 John 1:10 and say: "if we claim we are not forgiven, we make him out to be a liar and his word has no place in our lives." Have faith in God's mercy and grace.

When you start to feel like you have not been forgiven, read 1 John 1:9 and, if necessary, keep reading it until it sinks in. God, in His Holy Word, promises us that He will forgive us and purify us from *all* unrighteousness.

Always remember the great things about God's grace:

1. **You can be saved regardless:**
   ✥ No matter how old you are.
   ✥ No matter what sins you have committed.
   ✥ No matter how much you have sinned.
   ✥ No matter if you have not gone to church.
   ✥ No matter that you have previously denied or ignored God.
   ✥ No matter how rich or poor you are.
   ✥ No matter what color you are or what your nationality is.
   ✥ No matter how smart or knowledgeable you are.
2. **No sin is too great and it's not too late!**
3. **God's mercy and grace are infinite and free.**
4. **God's mercy and grace are always available.**

Remember: Salvation by Grace through Faith!

Selected Scripture
Romans 3:21-26; 5:1-2, 20; 11:6   Ephesians 1:5-7; 2:1-10
John 1:17   Titus 3:7   Hebrews 4:14-16

__Prayer__

Thank God for freely bestowing his gift of mercy and grace upon you and that you accept them without reservation.

Thank God for the freedom that His grace affords you – never having to worry whether you will measure up to a standard.

Thank God for the eternal destiny that His mercy and grace guarantee.

Ask God for the help of the Holy Spirit to live a righteous life and to convict you of your sins when you fall short.

Ask for protection from the flaming darts and accusations of Satan.

Day 20 – Love

The What

When we looked at the Holy Trinity, the point was made that the Triune Godhead was a distinguishing characteristic of Christianity. The other distinguishing aspect of Christianity is its basis on the love of God and on God's requirement for us to love Him and to love each other. God loves you, wants the best for you, and desires a personal relationship with you. Tozer states: "In Christian experience there is a highly satisfying love content that distinguishes it from all other religions and elevates it to heights far beyond even the purest and noblest philosophy." [1]

What can we say about God's love towards you?

1. God's love is free! God does not require you to earn His love. Ingram says: "He doesn't love us because of who we are but because of who he is. His nature and character compel him to express unconditional affection toward us." [2] God loves the saved and the unsaved – the righteous and the unrighteous. He just hates the sin!
2. God loves you unconditionally. He does not tell us He will love us only if…
3. God's love is an action towards you, not a reaction to you.
4. God's love towards you does not change. No matter if you change.

5. God loves you so that He can change you. God does not change you in order to love you.
6. God's love is always available. To this end, He is faithful.
7. God's love is infinite – absolutely limitless.
8. God's love is eternal – forever with Him in heaven. For the unsaved, however, God's goodness and love will not be present in hell.

God has revealed, or demonstrated, His love to us in so many ways. Let's look at a few:

How Revealed Or Demonstrated	What It Means to You
Made us in His image	You are special to God; you have special gifts and promises – but also special responsibilities.
His Son	With the gift of free will, God knew you would sin; yet He provided a way to redeem you to Him - a gift that flows from His love.
His Holy Spirit	God resides within you when you become a Christian and is always present for comfort, counseling and understanding.
His discipline	God uses selective correction to strengthen you and to protect you from self-destructive behavior.
His Holy Word	The Bible is a revelation of God's love for you. Consider it a love letter from God to you. See Appendix B.
As your Father	He desires to be close to you – a heavenly Daddy and child relation-ship. We are heirs to His eternal blessings.
As your friend	He has shared with you as friends, has revealed Himself to you as a

	friend, and sacrificed for you like a friend.
Rejoicing over you	God and His heavenly hosts rejoice over you when you repent and turn to Him. He rejoices over His children.
Through blessings	From a glorious creation to providing daily for your needs

So What?

Personalize God's Word to you so that you will really grasp its meaning and importance to you. Look at two of the great verses about love. "For God so loved *you* that He gave His one and only Son, that if *you* believe in Him, *you* will not perish but, instead, *you* will have eternal life." (paraphrased John 3:16) Quite a gift! Quite a promise! Also "But God demonstrates his own love for *you* in this: While *you* were still a sinner, Christ died for *you*. (paraphrased Romans 5:8) Even while you are rebellious, Christ's death is for you.

Focus on God's greatest commandments: to love Him and to love each other. Show your love for God by loving others. Let God's love live in you and through you. Let your love be a light to the world. Show the world you are Jesus' disciple through your love for others. Share God's love! Give it freely and unconditionally - asking nothing in return. Make your love for others an action – not a reaction to something good someone else has done for you.

Experience the fullness of God's love and what it will do for you. Great things will happen to you! Peace, joy, comfort and freedom! What a God you have!

Selected Scripture

Luke 6:27-36	John 14:23, 15:9-13	Mark 12:28-34
Hebrews 12:6, 10	Zephaniah 3:17	Luke 15:7
Romans 8:14-17		

Prayer

Pray Paul's prayer in Ephesians 3:17-19 for yourself, for your family and friends, and for others in the world. "And I pray that you, being rooted and established in love, may have power, together with all the saints, to grasp how wide and long and high and deep is the love of Christ, and to know this love that surpasses knowledge – that you may be filled to the measure of all the fullness of God."

Day 21 – Creative

The What

This lesson will not argue the case of creationism versus evolution. Genesis 1:1, "In the beginning God created the heavens and the earth" is assumed to be the absolute truth. Once you believe this one verse, then you can believe the rest of the Bible. Why do I think that? For God to have created and sustained this world and this universe, He would have to possess many of the attributes that we are discussing in this booklet. God has to be omnipotent, omniscient, omnipresent, creative, eternal, infinite, and sovereign. He had to have motivations such as love, majesty, and goodness. Miracles are essentially a "piece of cake" to God - else how could He have created such a vast, complex universe. You should not doubt such things as: healings, the resurrection, the raising of the dead, the flood, the parting of the Red Sea, dominion over earthly rulers, feeding the 5,000, turning water into wine, etc. - given you believe God created this universe. After accepting Genesis 1:1, the only issues with your faith should have to do with God's relationship to man. Let's look at a few examples (out of millions) of the awesome creativity of our God and just ask the question – how could this stuff just have happened. This material is taken from ***Creation: Remarkable Evidence of God's Design***, by Grant R. Jeffrey. (1)

The Human Eye
- After conception a million optic nerves start growing from the eye towards the optical section of the brain and simultaneously a million start growing from the brain to the eye; these will match up perfectly with their mates growing from the opposite direction.
- The retina is the most light sensitive object in the universe. Over 137,000,000 light sensitive cells – 95% for black and white and 5% for color – each of which is connected to an optic nerve.
- The retina cells perform up to 10 billion calculations per second and then transmit the images to the brain.
- The lens of the eye adjusts at incredible speed to accommodate different light intensities and moving objects.
- Even Darwin could not explain how evolution could have produced the eye.

The Cell
- Darwin had no means of knowing the complexity of the living cell, which was thought to be made up of some simple jelly-like substance. Now it is considered the most complex and beautiful system in the universe.
- There are trillions of cells in the body performing many different types of functions; these cells process and control thousands of chemicals and enzymes; each cell is protected by a membrane 1/3 of a millionth of an inch thick.
- Each cell is like a busy city performing functions like energy generation, defense against invaders, sophisticated communications, transportation, waste disposal, and factories producing nutrition.
- Each cell is more complicated than any supercomputer and any man-made machine – yet it is incredibly small.
- The information contained in the DNA in just one human cell would fill a library shelf over 100 yards long.

Beavers
- Beavers construct their dams at 45 degree angles – the same that is now used in all hydroelectric dam construction.

Honeybees
- The hexagonal structure of the honeycomb is the best possible geometric structure to maximize storage and inclined 13 degrees at the end to keep the honey from escaping. Tens of thousands of honeybees start simultaneously constructing the hives from 3 different points and directions – yet they are perfectly joined and constructed when completed. This astounds engineers.

Dolphins
- Dolphins possess sophisticated radar with sound wave vibrations of 200,000/second upon which the dolphin's brain performs many complex calculations instantaneously.
- The dolphin's snout is perfectly designed to minimize water resistance thereby enabling it to swim at incredible speeds. This design is now used on supertankers and military vessels.

Earth / Universe
- The earth is a planet perfectly designed to support life – just as Isaiah wrote in Isaiah 45:18.
- The earth is in the perfect location within the solar system, which is in the perfect location in the Milky Way galaxy, which is in the perfect location in the universe to support life on earth.
- The electrical communication in the 60 trillion cells in our body depends on the earth's magnetic field.
- The earth is the perfect distance from the sun, which is the perfect size and composition for the support of life.
- The earth has the perfect rotation and perfect tilting on its axis to support life.

- The moon is the perfect size and has the precise rotation around earth to support the tides which are essential to sustain life.
- The earth has the perfect atmospheric conditions to support life.
- The earth has an excellent supply of minerals and materials located near the earth's surface for man to use for his benefit.
- The electrical force that holds atoms together is precisely balanced and calibrated to allow the Universe to exist.

Do I need to get into the incredible variety of animal and plant life or the incredible balance within nature that sustains life? Think about the miracle of reproduction or the conscience and spirit within man. How about the beauty within nature, the majesty of a sunrise or sunset, the splendor of the Blue Ridge mountains, the breath-taking views of tropical islands and flowers? Then there is the ability of man to learn and apply God's gifts to his benefit. Or how about the incredible variety of fruits, vegetables, berries, spices, nuts, etc. for man to enjoy? Or cows and chickens that produce a surplus of eggs and milk for man? Or horses and other animals that are made to serve man? Or bees that produce honey - the perfect food? Wow – think about the love and care and goodness that God has shown towards man through His creation!!

So What?

Do not fall into the trap of believing in the God of the Bible and evolution. This is basically for double-minded people who are weak in their faith in the power of God and in His Holy Word. Place your trust in the Bible before placing your trust in the lies and false assumptions of men who cannot and will not accept God. If your need to bolster your faith against the academic world, you can read the following books:

The Case for a Creator, by Lee Strobel
Boyd's Handbook of Practical Apologetics, by Robert T. Boyd

Creation: Remarkable Evidence of God's Design, by Grant R. Jeffrey

Take time to marvel at the unbelievable beauty and complexity of God's creation. If you continually take these things for granted, then your respect for the majesty, power and knowledge of God diminishes.

Selected Scripture

Hebrews 11:3   By faith we understand that the universe was formed at God's command, so that what is seen was not made out of what was visible.

Psalm 19:1   The heavens declare the glory of God; the skies proclaim the works of his hands.

Psalm 139:13-14   For you created my inmost being; you knit me together in my mother's womb. I praise you because I am fearfully and wonderfully made; your works are wonderful, I know that full well.

Romans 1:20   For since the creation of the world God's invisible qualities - his eternal power and divine nature - have been clearly seen, being understood from what has been made, *so that men are without excuse*.

Proverbs 20:12   The hearing ear, and the seeing eye, the Lord hath made even both of them.

Isaiah 45:18   For this is what the Lord says - he who created the heavens; he is God; he who fash-ioned and made the earth, he founded it; he did not create it to be empty, but formed it to be inhabited - he says I am the Lord, and there is no other.

Prayer

Praise God for the incredible and awesome world He has given to us. Thank Him for His infinite love and goodness.
Thank God for being our provider and sustainer.

Day 22 – Worthy

The What

At an antique auction the bidding goes back and forth for an antique chest. The final, winning bid is $8,700. Is that the value, or true worth, of that piece of furniture? A house is put on the market for $189,000, but the actual agreed upon sell price is $181,500. What is the real value of that property? On March 6, 2006 the price per barrel of light crude oil closes at $63.27; the price for a troy ounce of gold closes at $570.60; and the price for corn closes at 239.25 cents per bushel. Is that the true value or worth for these commodities? A set of steak knives, whose value is $99.00 according to the advertiser, can be bought right now in this special TV offer for 2 easy payments of $14.99 (plus $7.99 shipping and handling). Is the value $99.00, or $29.98, or $37.97? The classic answer an economist would give is to say the value is determined by the marketplace. What is the market willing to pay and what is the owner willing to sell for? What is the agreed upon price? This value will, however, be affected by the participants in the market and by the conditions at that point in time. For example, an antiques expert might look at the chest and know that it is worth $18,000 because of who made it and how old it is. In each of the above cases the value is not determined by what the seller says it is, nor does the buyer establish the true value. The value will vary for any number of reasons, such as: economic conditions, the buyer's desire at that moment to possess that item, some piece of local or world news, a terrorist attack, other suppliers, how many buyers there are, etc. The value of anything will depend on the perceived value to the buyer, and this perceived value will vary over time. How much is it worth to you, the buyer? Maybe you would have been willing to pay $200,000 for the house because it had just what you were looking for. Maybe you would have purchased the steak knives if the price was $10.00 less.

Well, God is not like any of the above items. God is worthy because HE IS WHO HE IS. God is infinitely worthy, 100% of the time, for all eternity. God does not change. God is infinitely and eternally worthy; because God is infinitely and eternally good, loving, merciful, gracious, majestic, wise, omnipotent, omniscient, omnipresent, holy, just, patient, sovereign, divine, compassionate, honest and faithful. He is the Creator and Sustainer of all things. His worthiness does not depend on how much value you place on Him, just like His existence is independent of your belief in Him. Whether you believe in Him, or not, has nothing to do with whether He exists. Whether you believe He is worthy, or not, has nothing to do with His worthiness. Your view of God's worthiness only determines what is in your heart, nothing more – nothing less. Two key verses of Scripture spoken by Christ address this very point:

Matthew 6:21   **For where your treasure is, your heart will be also.**

Matthew 16:26   **What good will it be for a man if he gains the whole world, yet forfeits his soul? Or what can a man give in exchange for his soul?**

These verses reflect on two critical thoughts. First, even though you do not determine God's true worthiness, you do determine how much value and worth God has in your own heart and soul. God knows how worthy you deem Him to be. Second, everyone places a certain value on their eternal soul. Jesus clearly states that you should value your eternal soul and spirit more than all of the wealth known to man. How you view God, how you respond to God, and how you value your relationship to God defines the value you place on your eternal soul.

So What?

First of all, do not let outside influences affect the worth you place on your relationship to God. Be careful not to let your faith and perception of God be influenced by so-called scholars or scoffers. Know that what these people write or say means **_nothing_**. Instead, focus on the worthiness of God as portrayed by the picture of Him given to us in the Bible. Come to know God through studying His Word and through passionate prayer and worship.

Focus on the worthiness of Christ and the **_real value_** of His sacrifice on the cross. Two important questions everyone should ask themselves are:

- In my heart, what worth have I placed on Jesus Christ?
- Does my life reflect this?

Hopefully, one key result of this 40-day study is that by knowing God better, the worthier He will become in your own life. Perhaps you may come to the realization that you cannot even begin to grasp His true worthiness. Then you will desire to glorify God by reflecting His worthiness in your daily living through:

- Worship,
- Praise,
- Adoration and love,
- Obedience, and
- Service.

Selected Scripture
1 Chronicles 16:25
and Psalm 96:4   For great is the Lord and most worthy of praise; he is to be feared above all gods.

2 Samuel 22:4 and Psalm 18:3	I call to the Lord, who is worthy of praise, and I am saved from my enemies.
Psalm 145:3	Great is the Lord and most worthy of praise; his greatness no one can fathom.
Revelation 4:9-11	worthy is God the Father
Revelation 5:6-14	worthy is God the Son

Prayer

Praise God for He is worthy.

Thank God, that even though you are unworthy, He still bestows His infinite love and goodness and grace upon you.

Commit yourself to a life more worthy of His blessings.

Day 23 – Jealous

The What

We are inclined to have negative thoughts when we hear the word jealousy. Webster defines jealous as "intolerant of rivalry or unfaithfulness". Jealousy should not be confused with the word "envious". God is not envious of other gods, or green with envy, or spiteful. God is truly intolerant of unfaithfulness to Him and does not want you to put anything ahead of Him. He wants no rivals in your life. God wants you to put Him number one in your life and to worship Him <u>only</u>. Period. This is straightforward; so none of us should be confused or try to offer excuses to God.

This leads us to ask about jealousy in our lives. Is jealousy always wrong in our lives? Let's look at a few examples where jealousy might not be wrong:

1. Is jealousy wrong when a wife expects her husband to be faithful to her? Or vice versa for the husband to expect faithfulness from the wife?
2. Is it wrong for a person to want to be the most important person to his/her spouse?
3. As a teenager, would jealous feelings be wrong if your girlfriend or boyfriend dated someone else behind your back?
4. How would you feel if your best friend betrayed you and did something to hurt you just to impress someone else?

I think we can agree that in each of these cases a person might be jealous. Is this jealousy good or bad? The motivation behind the jealousy is the determining factor as to whether the jealousy is good or bad. Is the jealousy based on love, trust and faithfulness; or is the jealousy rooted in that person's pride and selfishness? The Bible tells us that the husband/wife relationship is the single most important human relationship we will have. Jealousy based on spousal love and on respect for that relationship is not only good, but probably healthy as well.

Similarly, our relationship to God is the most important relationship we will have – even more so than with our spouse. God is jealous 100% of the time for this relationship; but His jealousy is 100% pure, because His motives are pure. God desires what is best for us, and He knows separation from Him is not good for us. God's goodness, love, mercy, grace, faithfulness and omniscience all interact to make His jealousy holy and pure. Just like all of God's attributes, you cannot look at jealousy without considering how all of God's attributes work together to comprise the fullness of God.

On the other hand, when we look at all of the wonderful things God has done for us, it is easy to fall into the trap of believing God has earned the "right" to be jealous. God created man in His image, and we exist for His glory. Everything we have, God has provided. God loves us and has promised us unbelievable, eternal blessings with Him. All of these are great, but God is jealous because HE IS WHO HE IS, not because of what He does. When we see God as the awesome and majestic God He is, we will not view His jealousy as a negative.

God's holiness and jealousy are attributes we must know and understand God to have a complete picture of Him as presented in the Bible. Ignoring these attributes can lead us to an attitude where we ignore and disobey God without any concern for His wrath. Listen to what J. I Packer has to say about those that would deny God's jealousy and wrath. He calls it "Santa Claus theology".

"But on the basis of the Santa Claus theology, sins create no problem, and atonement becomes needless; God's active favor (grace) extends no less to those who disregard his commands than to those who keep them. The idea that God's attitude to me is affected by whether or not I do what he says has no place in the thought of the man on the street, and any attempt to show the need for fear in God's presence, for trembling at his word, gets written off as impossibly old-fashioned – "Victorian", "Puritan" and "sub-Christian."" (1)

God's wrath has and will come down upon man. The Jews experienced it; the Canaanites experienced it; the Egyptians experienced it; the cities of Sodom, Gomorrah, and Tyre experienced it. At the end times, the whole world will experience it – those that have not been raptured. His wrath stems from His jealousy and His holiness but is caused by man's rejection of Him and by man's sin. God is jealous, so He hates being rejected; God is holy, so He detests sin. The result is God's anger and wrath. These should cause you to fear God, but that is what the Bible states is the beginning of wisdom.

To put this in perspective as Christians: if God is not jealous and wrathful and if He does not judge sins, then Christ's death and resurrection have no meaning. "For the substance of Christianity is faith in the forgiveness of sins through the redeeming work of Christ on the cross." (2) If we deny God's jealousy and wrathfulness, then "Christianity…simply dies off." (3)

So What?

God's jealousy should not be viewed as a weakness, or flaw, in His character. His jealousy is rightly justified simply because of who He is. God's jealousy, along with His holiness, is a reason for us to fear the Lord God. However, His jealousy should also serve as a motivation to put Him first in our lives to worship Him only.

Examine the Ten Commandments in Exodus 20, and you will find that the first four deal with our relationship with God. God's jealousy is the reason for the first two commandments. That should tell each of us the importance of having God first in our lives and honoring Him.

In our personal lives, remember our own jealousy can be good or bad. When jealousy stems from coveting something or someone else, then it is bad. Jealousy based on expectations of love, trust and faithfulness are good and are very much like the God in whose image we are created.

Selected Scripture
Exodus 20:3-6; 34:6-7   Deuteronomy 6:13-18   Psalm 37:13

Prayer
Acknowledge God's jealousy.

Pray to God to help you identify anything that prevents Him from being first in your life.

Pray for God's guidance and help in overcoming this sin.

Praise God for His love, mercy and grace which keeps you from His wrath.

Day 24 – Holy and Righteous

The What

A discussion of God's holiness cannot help but be theological; but now is the time you need to focus and really dwell on the Holy nature of God. Nothing can be as important as truly understanding God's holiness. So as you read this lesson concentrate and meditate.

In the Book of Isaiah alone, God is referred to as "the Holy One" about 30 times. Of all the attributes we are going to discuss, *holy* is the most important and yet perhaps the most difficult to comprehend. William Evans stated, "If any distinction at all can be made between the attributes of God – whether omnipotence, omnipresence, omniscience, etc. – the *divine holiness* is the one attribute which God would have His people think of as standing out above all the others." (1) In addition, A. W. Tozer, who is one of the most qualified theologians of the past one hundred years, wrote, "Neither the writer nor the reader of these words is qualified to appreciate the holiness of God." (2)

When we say God is holy, we mean that He is completely separate from evil and is the total absence of anything evil. God is absolute moral excellence and perfection. To be holy, truly holy, God must be 100% pure – not even 99.9999999% pure will suffice. To paraphrase Tozer, the divine holiness of God does not conform to a standard we can comprehend or imagine – it is THE STANDARD. (3)

"This perfection, as none other, is solemnly celebrated before the Throne of Heaven, the seraphim crying, **"Holy, holy, holy, is the Lord of hosts"** (Isaiah 6:3)." (4) The cry is not: "Love,   love, love, is the Lord of hosts" or

"Majestic, majestic, majestic is the Lord of hosts" or
"Wise, wise, wise is the Lord of hosts" or
"Sovereign, sovereign, sovereign is the Lord of hosts".

The Lord God has the seraphim praising His holiness above anything else.

"God Himself singles out this perfection, **"Once for all, I have sworn by my holiness – and I will not lie to David."** (Psalm 89:35 NIV). God swears by His holiness because that is a *fuller* expression of Himself than anything else." (5)

Arthur Pink had these tough words to say: "Because God is holy He *hates all sin*. … It follows, therefore, that He must necessarily *punish sin*. Sin can no more exist without demanding His punishment than without requiring His hatred of it. God has often forgiven sinners, but He never forgives sin; and the sinner is only forgiven on the ground of Another (Jesus) having borne his punishment; for **"without the shedding of blood there is no forgiveness"** (Hebrews 9:22)". (6)

So What?

There are several critical points that we as Christians must understand. First, the main theme of the Bible is based on God's holiness, man's sin, and the redemption of man to God through the payment of sin by Jesus Christ. Without a basic understanding of God's holiness the whole foundation and underlying beliefs of Christianity fall apart. We must understand that our sin separates us from a Holy God. Man's sin and God's holiness, in essence, are why we need a Savior and Redeemer. Man is not and cannot be holy on his own. We will all stand before God – either stained by our sins or completely clean and stain free. Faith in the grace of the shed blood of Jesus allows us to confidently appear before the Holy God cleansed of our sins. This is God's gift to us, yet so many find it hard to accept this gift because of such reasons as:

1. They already feel worthy on their on merits. These people feel they are "good enough".
2. They want a checklist or something they can measure.
3. Putting faith in the holy God requires a person to give up some things that are just too appealing, and selfish desires keep them from accepting the gift.
4. Pride keeps some people from humbling themselves before God.
5. Some people just get caught up in the present day activities and demands and do not give serious consideration to the matter.

When we begin to understand God's holiness, we begin to see why we need salvation. Why we need to repent and ask forgiveness. Why we need to believe that Jesus' death was adequate payment for our sins. It will also allow us to see why there is only one way to heaven – and that is the way God has provided, Jesus Christ.

Second, God's holiness was terrifying to those chosen few in the Bible that were allowed the honor of experiencing His holiness. These men were as holy as men will ever be – yet they were terrified in the presence of the Holy God. Isaiah cried out, **"Woe is me!"**; Daniel, John and Paul all fell prostate and fainted. We need to have a *reverent fear* of a Holy God, which will result in sincere repentance and earnest prayers. In Proverbs and Psalms we read several times that **"The fear of the Lord is the beginning of knowledge"** – and, I believe, the beginning of the knowledge of the Holy One. This fear is a good fear that creates worship and will draw us closer to Him as we also experience His grace, love and forgiveness. Let me pose this question, can you imagine a god that is not holy? A god that was omnipotent, omnipresent, omniscient, jealous, etc. without being also holy would be like the devil with unlimited power, with no desire of good things for you. Now that would be reason for horrific terror. But the God of the Bible is holy and worthy of praise and glory. Can I get a big AMEN?

Third, being holy is the goal of our obedience to God. Jesus said, **"Be perfect, therefore, as your heavenly Father is perfect."** Jesus knew man could not be perfect on his own, but through faith in Him we could be made perfect. See Hebrews 10:14-17 and Romans 4:5-8 for your assurance of righteousness and holiness before God. These are great verses! Jesus expects us to strive to be holy and produce good fruit during our lives. The true evidence that you are a disciple of Christ and a child of God is the fruit you bear; and you bear good fruit through obedience, holy living and service to God.

Selected Scripture

Exodus 15:11   "Who among the gods is like you, O Lord? Who is like you – majestic in holiness, awesome in glory, working wonders?"

Proverbs 9:10   "The fear of the Lord is the beginning of wisdom, and knowledge of the Holy One is understanding."

Isaiah 6:3   "Holy, holy, holy is the Lord Almighty; the whole earth is full of His glory."

Isaiah 6:5   "Woe to me!" I cried. "I am ruined! For I am a man of unclean lips, and I live among a people of unclean lips, and my eyes have seen the King, the Lord Almighty."

Revelation 4:8   "Holy, holy, holy is the Lord God Almighty, who was, and is, and is to come."

Revelation 15:4   "Who will not fear you, O Lord, and bring glory to your name? For you alone are holy. All nations will come and worship before you, for you righteous acts have been revealed."

Psalm 96:9   "Worship the Lord in the splendor of his holiness; tremble before him, all the earth."

Isaiah 8:13   "The Lord Almighty is the one you are to regard as holy, he is the one you are to fear, He is the one you are to dread."

Isaiah 59:2	"But your sins have made a separation between you and your God."
Matthew 5:48	"Be perfect, therefore, as your heavenly Father is perfect."
1 Peter 1:13-16	"Therefore prepare your minds for action; be self-controlled; set your hope fully on the grace to be given you when Jesus Christ is revealed. As obedient children, do not conform to the evil desires you had when you lived in ignorance. But just as he who called you is holy, so be holy in all you do; for it is written: "Be holy, because I am holy.""
Hebrews 12:10	"God disciplines us for our own good, that we may share in his holiness."
Hebrews 12:14	"Make every effort to live in peace with all men and to be holy; without holiness no one will see the Lord."
1 John 1:5	"… God is light; in him there is no darkness at all."

Other Scripture Readings

Hebrews 10: 14-17	Jesus makes us perfect and holy by His sacrifice
Romans 4:5-8	Our faith is credited as righteousness
Galatians 5:19-25	Evidence of sin versus evidence of the fruit of the Spirit working in us

Prayer

Praise God for His holiness.

Pray for the Holy Spirit to help you understand God's holiness.

Pray for the Holy Spirit to work in your life so that you can overcome temptations and live more holy and obedient.

Day 25 – Sovereign

The What

Webster defines sovereignty as having supreme authority or power over something. As free Americans we might have a hard time truly grasping what a sovereign ruler can mean. Saddam Hussein (Iraq) and Kim Il Sung (North Korea) have had as much sovereignty as any rulers during recent times. When Hussein first came to power in 1979, he held a meeting with members of his government. There in a large hall, individuals were taken out one by one to be tortured and killed. Their crime was that Saddam thought they might pose a threat to his dictatorship. Those that remained would forever be too frightened to question Hussein and were forever grateful to have been spared. Over the years Hussein used his supreme power to live in incredible wealth, building many palaces worth hundreds of millions of dollars. Torture chambers were in frequent use as he squashed any apparent threat. He started a war with Iran that resulted in the deaths of millions. He and his sons had any woman they chose – often just picking them up off the street to satisfy themselves. Saddam used chemical weapons to kill thousands that were not part of the Bathe Party or Sunni faith. He had his army invade Kuwait in order to fuel his desire for more power and wealth. He was a living example of a truth that applies to mankind - "Absolute power corrupts absolutely." Fortunately, Hussein and others are limited by time, breadth of dominion, and other people.

Their power is limited to what God has allowed through His sovereignty.

There are three key thoughts that we should consider in regards to sovereignty.

First, God is absolutely sovereign over His entire creation. He rules 100% of the time over 100% of everything that exists. In other words, God is not semi-sovereign over His creation – just like a woman cannot be semi-pregnant. God can be absolutely sovereign; because He is omniscient, omnipresent, omnipotent, self-existent, self-sufficient, infinite and eternal. He is totally independent from anything in existence and absolutely free to do as He pleases.

Second, God takes responsibility for all that happens in His creation – both good and bad. Just look at three verses that specifically address this:

Exodus 4:11	**"The Lord said to him, "Who gave man his mouth? Who makes him deaf or mute? Who gives him sight or makes him blind? Is it not I, the Lord?""**
Isaiah 45:7	**I form the light and create darkness; I bring prosperity and create disaster; I, the Lord, do all these things.**
John 9:3	And Jesus responding to His disciples about a blind man said: **"Neither this man nor his parents sinned", said Jesus, "but this happened so that the work of God might be displayed in his life."**

Sometimes God directly causes some bad things to happen; and sometimes the suffering is self-inflicted, but God still allows the suffering to happen. God could thwart evil at any time, but He still allows it to continue for now. We must understand and have faith that God has a purpose, even though we may not understand it.

Third, understand that God's absolute power and sovereignty are ultimately good, because His overall plan and will are driven by all of His attributes. God tells us that He is good, loving and merciful. Robert Jeffress makes a statement that fits the whole thrust behind this 40-day journey:

"Real faith is believing that God is who He says He is even when in the darkness we can't see that goodness." (1)

Another question that arises when we talk about God's sovereignty is: If God is totally sovereign, then how can man have free will or the freedom to choose? I like the example A. W. Tozer used to explain how God's sovereignty and man's free will exist together.

"An ocean liner leaves New York bound for Liverpool. Its destination has been determined by proper authorities. Nothing can change it. This is at least a faint picture of sovereignty.

On board the liner are several scores of passengers. These are not in chains, neither are their activities determined for them by decree. They are completely free to move about as they will. They eat, sleep, play, lounge about on the deck, read, talk, altogether as they please; but all the while the great liner is carrying them steadily onward toward a predetermined port.

Both freedom and sovereignty are present here and they do not contradict each other. So it is, I believe, with man's freedom and the sovereignty of God. The mighty liner of God's sovereign design keeps its steady course over the sea of history. God moves undisturbed and unhindered toward the fulfillment of those eternal purposes which He purposed in Christ Jesus before the world began. We do not know all that is included in those purposes, but enough has been disclosed to furnish us with a broad outline of things to come and to give us good hope and firm assurance of future well-being." (2)

So What?

Let's look at what God's sovereignty means to all mankind and to us personally. God is in control. He has purposed for things to happen as they have and as they will; and there is nothing any person can do to change that. This creation is moving towards the finality that God has revealed in His Word. The present imperfect world that we know will be destroyed, and a new heaven and earth will be created. Those who choose, under their free will, to live in darkness will be sentenced to hell. Those who choose to accept God's plan of salvation will be with God in heaven forever. There will be a winning side and a losing side in this conflict of holiness versus evil. See Appendix E – Choice.

None of us can understand God's reasons and thoughts, but you must have faith in His <u>total</u> Being – especially in times of suffering. Have faith in God's wisdom and goodness. Have faith that God uses short-term suffering for the purpose of accomplishing long-term good. Do not let the sufferings of this temporary world separate you from focusing on God's eternal plan.

Selected Scripture
Daniel 4:34-35   Isaiah 46:8-11   Psalm 22:28; 103:8; 107:1
Philippians 2:13

Prayer
Acknowledge God's sovereign control over creation.
Praise His holiness and goodness which mean His sovereignty guarantees you good things.
Ask for as much understanding of God's plan as the Holy Spirit will reveal when going through suffering or trials, pray that God will use this to draw you closer to Him.
Pray for the help of the Holy Spirit to prevent suffering from separating you from God.

Day 26 - Father

The What

We are going to culminate our discussion about God's attributes with God as Father, because of its importance in truly understanding what a Christian is. How would you define a Christian? Pause and think about that, before reading further. Maybe you came up with a lengthy description that has to do with accepting Jesus Christ as your Lord and Savior, repenting of your sins, and maybe some other related thoughts. None of these would be incorrect. However, J. I. Packer provides one of the simplest, yet maybe one of the richest definitions – "a Christian is one who has God as Father". (1) Packer went on to say: "If you want to judge how well a person understands Christianity, find out how much he makes of the thought of being God's child, and having God as his Father." (2)

Not everyone is a child of God. Some people would disagree with this statement. They might be thinking that since God created all people, He is the Father of everyone. No, He is the Creator of all things; but He is the Father only to those who have been born again, by a "spiritual conception". A person cannot truly know God as Father unless he/she has been drawn to Him and received His gift of salvation. John 1:12-13 states:

> **Yet to all who received him, to those who believed in his name, he gave the right to become <u>children of God</u> – chil-**

dren born not of natural descent, nor of human decision or a husband's will, but born of God."

"Sonship to God, then, is a gift of grace." (3) We are not natural children, but adoptive children of God.

In the Old Testament, the theme is on the holiness of God and how man's sin separated him from God. The relationship of man to God focuses on man's fear of God and reverence towards God. There is not as much closeness to God as there is total awe of God. None of these are bad or wrong; they are simply changed in the New Testament with the new covenant that comes through Christ. Christians become sons and daughters of God – heirs that inherit the blessings of His eternal kingdom; and Father is the name by which God is now known. "And the stress of the New Testament is not on the difficulty and danger of drawing near to the holy God, but on the boldness and confidence with which believers may approach him: a boldness that springs directly from faith in Christ, and from the knowledge of his saving work." (4) One of my favorite verses is Ephesians 3:12:

"In him and through faith in him we may approach God with freedom and confidence."

"To those who are Christ's, the holy God is a loving Father; they belong to his family; they approach him without fear and always be sure of his fatherly concern and care. This is the heart of the New Testament message." (5)

Jesus referred to God as Father 167 times in the Gospels. He told us God was our Father most clearly in the model prayer (or Lord's Prayer) when he began the prayer "Our Father who art in heaven…". Jesus also said in John 20:17:

"…Go instead to my brothers and tell them, "I am returning to my Father and your Father, to my God and your God."

That is about as clear as it can possibly be. Not only did Jesus say God was your Father and mine, but that we are His brothers (and sisters). Again in Mark 3:34-35 Jesus states:

"Then he looked at those seated in a circle around him and said, "Here are my mother and my brothers! Whoever does God's will is my brother and sister and mother.""

So What?

Think about this one fact: one day (either by your earthly death or by rapture) you will stand before the Lord God. As a Christian, you will be a child of God meeting your Father face-to-face. If you are not saved, you will be a sin-stained person facing your Judge. God will not be your Father.

Think about how truly blessed being a child of God makes you. To be justified before God means you are forgiven of your sins and will not be punished or held liable for them. That is wonderful news, but it does not signify a close personal relationship with God. As an adopted child of God you get to experience God's love, fellowship and generosity. "To be right with God the Judge is a great thing, but to be loved and cared for by God the Father is greater." (6) It is the *"highest privilege the gospel offers."* (7)

Maybe you are not (or were not) blessed to have a close relationship with your earthly father. I hope you were. But know that Scripture tells us that God not only wants to be our Father, but a close loving Father – a Daddy. That is what is meant in Scripture when we are told we can call out Abba. Having had a great Dad on earth – well now that really means something special to me. In either case, I hope it does to you as well!

Selected Scripture
Romans 8:12-17   Galatians 3:26-4:7   1 John 3:1-3

Prayer
Go to God as your Father, your Daddy, and pray to Him as such.
Talk with God about your personal problems and needs.
Tell God you love Him.

What Are Some Examples of How God's Attributes Have Been Revealed?

Day 27 – The Ten Commandments

The What

Have you ever considered how the Ten Commandments reveal the nature of God? Too often people see the Ten Commandments simply as a set of rules and regulations for man to follow. A fuller understanding, however, will take us beyond the black and white of laws and allow us to peek into the mind and heart of God. Let's travel in our minds back to a day and place about 3400 years ago to one of the most incredible events in history. What an awesome scene!

> **"On the morning of the third day there was thunder and lightening with a thick cloud over the mountain, and a very loud trumpet blast. Everyone in the camp trembled. Then Moses led the people out of the camp to meet with God, and they stood at the foot of the mountain. Mount Sinai was covered with smoke, because the Lord descended on it in fire. The smoke billowed up from it like smoke from a furnace, the whole mountain trembled violently, and the sound of the trumpet grew louder and louder. There Moses spoke and the voice of God answered him. The Lord descended to the top of Mount Sinai and called Moses to the top of the mountain. So Moses went up..."** (Exodus 19:16-20)

This was the holy and majestic scene in which God chose to speak the Ten Commandments to Moses and inscribe them with His finger on two stone tablets. There are more to them than just ten hard-and-fast rules for us to follow.

To understand the impact of the Ten Commandments and how they go beyond being just a simple set of rules, let's examine a two-way mirror and how it works. On one side of the mirror you see your reflection; and looking into the other side of the mirror, you can see through it into the room on the other side. Likewise, the Ten Commandments are a "spiritual two-way mirror". From one side we can look into the mind and heart, the very nature, of God. The first four commandments tell us that God wants to have a relationship with each of us. God wants us to know He is **omnipotent** and **sovereign** and expects obedience. God is **holy** and **righteous** and wants man, whom He made in His image, to know and respect these attributes. God tells us He is a **jealous** God, and He demands to be number one in our lives and be the only focus of our worship. God deems Himself to be **worthy** of our total respect and of our worship. God tells us that we are to live lives that bring **glory** to Him through our obedience to His holy and righteous laws. God wants what is **good** for us; and, because of His **omniscience** and **perfect wisdom**, He can define a code of conduct that will result in good lives for mankind. We are told in Deuteronomy 6 that the commandments are for us to enjoy a long life and so that life may go well with us. Think about how much better the world would be if we all adhered to the Ten Commandments. In Matthew 22:36-40 Jesus summarized the Ten Commandments in two simple statements about loving God and loving each other. The Ten Commandments aptly and simply demonstrate God's **love** for us and His desire for His creation to live and be ruled by **love**.

Now let's go to the other side of the spiritual mirror and read the Ten Commandments. What do you see? The spiritual mirror reflects our wickedness and sinfulness. We understand that if we are judged by these commandments that we are all guilty of sin. The Ten Commandments are not intended to save man from God's wrath; but, instead, they point directly towards the need for a Savior that will reconcile us to a holy God. The Ten Commandments, and our inability to follow them completely, help us to recognize the need for God's *mercy* and *grace*. God has given each of us the gift of salvation and redemption by faith in Jesus – we just have to believe it and receive it.

During His life on earth as our Rabboni, Jesus expanded the depth, meaning and application of the commandments. He tells us to examine not only our actions, but our thoughts and motives as well. He expands "murder" to include anger and hate, and He expands adultery to include lustful thoughts. Christ knows that what is in your heart and mind might eventually lead to action. In Luke 6:27-36 and Luke 18:18-25 Jesus goes even further in expanding the commandments by saying that not only should we not do bad things but that we should do good things for others.

So What?

Look at and study the spiritual two-way mirror often – from both sides. God put on a real fireworks show when He gave us the Ten Commandments. They are important to Him. Just read the following verses in Deuteronomy 6:6-8:

"These commandments that I give you today are to be upon your hearts. Impress them on your children. Talk to them when you sit at home and when you walk along the road, when you lie down and when you get up. Tie them as symbols on your hands and bind them on your foreheads. Write them on the doorframes of your houses and on your gates."

We are told in Proverbs 3:3 and 7:3 to **"write them on the tablet of your heart."**

I think we can agree that they are important to God and, therefore, should be important to us.

Understand that God's commandments are just as relevant to us today as they were to the Jewish people. These laws are permanent, absolute truths that we can live by today, because the God of the Bible is *immutable* – the same yesterday, today and tomorrow.

Understand that we have a solution to the problem that the Ten Commandments create. The solution to the problem is Jesus Christ and the grace available through His salvation. Remember, Jesus came into the world to fulfill the Law, not to abolish it.

Selected Scripture
Exodus 20:1-17   Deuteronomy 6:1-9
Matthew 5:17-19; 22:36-40
Romans 8:1-11   Galatians 2:15-21; 3:5-14

Prayer
Thank God for His commandments that has served mankind through thousands of years of changing governments and nations.
Praise God for His grace and mercy that is available to each of us, because no man can live free of sin.
Pray for the Holy Spirit to inscribe the Commandments on the tablet of your heart.

Day 28 – Parable of the Prodigal Son

The What

Take a few minutes to read Luke 15:11-32. This is a really great parable that Jesus told to the sinners gathered around Him and to the Pharisees who were muttering: **"This man welcomes sinners and eats with them." (Luke 15:2)** Jesus wanted them all to know what God is really like.

I have always restricted my thinking regarding this parable to God the Father, but it is truly representative of the *Trinity* of God acting in unison. God has taken the initiative to reconcile man to Him through Jesus Christ and the work of the Holy Spirit. Just as the son reflected on his sins, the Holy Spirit convicts us of our sins and reveals the truth to us. Just as the father humbled himself and ran out to meet his son and to kiss him, Jesus was God incarnate, who humbled Himself and came down and out to meet us, to reach out to us with open arms and to reconcile us to God.

Let's examine a few of the attributes of God that are very evident in the parable:

Compassionate	The father is concerned and cares about his lost child. The father keeps an eye out for the son, longing for him to return.
Patience	The father waits patiently for his son to return.

Unconditional love	The father's love was unconditional. His love did not depend on anything the son did, nor did his love cease after the son rejected him.
Unlimited grace	The father accepts the son back into the family, not because he thought the son had been punished enough and not because he figured the son now had learned hard, valuable lessons at the school of hard knocks and would not ever do something wrong again. He did not accept the son back and require him to earn the father's love and grace. The acceptance by the father was because of the father's unlimited grace and nothing else. A ring, sandals, the best robe, a feast – talk about unmerited favor.
Mercy	The father did not punish the son – even though he was selfish, rejected the father, and foolishly squandered his inheritance. Even the son believed the just thing for the father would be to treat him as a servant, not as his child.
Fatherly love	The father rejoiced when the lost son returned. God rejoices over you as a person – as His child. He also rejoices with his whole family - heaven and all the saints rejoice!
Sovereign	The father was in control and had the power to choose how he responded. His actions were based on decisions he made. The father could have denied the son when the son asked for his share of the inheritance. God is sovereign and in control. However, he has

granted man free will and choices, along with the responsibilities that go with them.

So What?

Take heart in the fact that God will accept you into His family, no matter how lost you are and no matter how dirty and smelly your sins have made you. No matter how bad your sins have been or how many sins you have committed, God's grace does not have to be earned – in fact, it cannot be earned. God's grace is freely given to those who truly repent in their hearts and trust God's gift of Jesus as their Savior.

God grieves over your lost soul and rejoices when you earnestly repent and come to Him. **"because this brother of yours was dead and is alive again; he was lost and is found." (Luke 15:32)** What an absolutely wonderful, mind-boggling thought! The Almighty God of the universe rejoices when you repent, come to Him, and accept His gift of grace.

Just as illustrated in this parable, God's forgiveness is an action (not an attribute) based on two things:

1. God is *love*; God is *good*; God is *merciful*; and God is *gracious*. Remember – He Is Who He Is.
2. The son "comes to his senses", that is he responds to the prompting of the Holy Spirit, and takes the initiative to go to his father for forgiveness. He repents, which means that not only was he truly sorry for his sins but that he also turned away from the sins and turned to his father.

Just as in this parable God has a celebration feast planned for you. **"Blessed are those who are invited to the wedding supper of the Lamb!" (Revelation 19:9)**

A key message of this Parable (from Adrian Rogers) is:

*No one is so bad as to keep them from heaven (younger
  son),*
and
*No one is so good as to merit automatic inclusion (older
  son).*

Selected Scripture
Luke 15:11-32   2 Peter 3:9   Revelation 19:6-9

Prayer
Thank God that His love for you is so great that He reaches out to
you.
Thank God for His patience and grace and for the supper He has
planned for you.

Day 29 – Healing of the Woman

The What

Take a couple of minutes to read Mark 5:21-34.

In this story, Jesus has just healed the man possessed by many demons. Jesus did not let the man follow Him, but instead had the man go home and witness. In verse 19 Jesus says, "Go home to your family and tell them how much the **Lord** has done for you, and how he has had **mercy** on you." Several of God's attributes (***omnipotence, mercy, sovereignty, compassion, glory, divinity***) had clearly been seen by the large crowd which gathered around Him by the lake. Even a synagogue ruler, Jairus, acknowledges Jesus' ***divine power*** and expresses faith in Jesus' ***mercy and goodness***. Jairus acknowledges the ***worthiness*** of Jesus. As Jesus goes on His way with Jairus to heal his daughter, a woman moves through the crowd just hoping to touch Jesus' clothes and be healed. Here is what we can ascertain / assume about this woman:

1. She has been sick and has suffered for twelve years.
2. She is now poor – having spent all she had trying to be cured. This gives a good indication of her degree of suffering.
3. She would have been considered unclean by the Jewish community and would have been estranged from the community. She would have had no relationships during this time. She probably suffered emotionally as well as physically.

4. She would have been considered a lower class person, much lower on the ladder of importance than Jairus.

5. She was very courageous, or had incredible faith, or was very determined, or was very desperate. She was probably all of these. This woman broke a lot of society's codes and social taboos. Here is a woman, an unclean woman, which touched another person (a man, a holy man at that) in public.

So what do we see in Jesus and how He responded to this woman. First, we see Jesus' *divine power* at work when the woman is healed. Jesus, just as God the Father did as far back as with Adam and Eve in the Garden, asked the crowd a question for which He already knew the answer: "Who touched my clothes?" I propose that Jesus knew the woman was in the crowd and was going to touch Him prior to her actually doing it. His *omniscience* was demonstrated to the crowd so that they would have another reason to believe. Jesus kept looking around waiting (*patiently*) for the woman to admit what she had done. Jesus did this for her benefit and for the benefit of the crowd. The woman was afraid but confessed her actions and told the whole truth. Then in one of the great verses in the Bible that reflects so much about our God, Jesus tells the woman: **"Daughter, your faith has healed you. Go in peace and be freed from your suffering."** Jesus shows *mercy, love and compassion* towards this woman, not in just healing her physically but in the way He treated her. In this response Jesus has elevated the status of this woman from lowly to blessed. Without directly saying it, Jesus forgave her violation of social taboos and freed the woman from guilt. Jesus was *just* in how He treated the woman, because He saw worth in her. The woman's status did not matter to Jesus; He still *loved* her and showed her respect. But notice the first word that Jesus spoke to her. He called her daughter. Jesus was clearly stating the *Father* – child relationship that God desires for us. He wants us to have a direct connection with Him. Even sick and lowly people can be the children of God. In this one simple story we see the power of Jesus heal the woman physically, emotionally, relationally, and spiritually.

So What?

Just as Jesus rewarded the woman's faith, He will reward you and bless you for your faith. Just as Jesus forgave the woman, He will forgive you and free you from your guilt. Just like the woman, your faith in Jesus Christ will bring you peace.

This woman overcame her feelings of unworthiness and took initiative to seek out the Lord. You must not allow any feelings that you have about your current status interfere with your relationship to Jesus Christ. Do not let past sins and your feelings of being too dirty and unclean prevent you from reaching out to touch Jesus.

Selected Scripture
Mark 5:21-34

Prayer
Praise God for His power and mercy to heal us emotionally, spiritually and physically.

Acknowledge your sins and ask God to forgive your sins, cleanse you and make you worthy before God.

If appropriate, pray for physical and emotional healing for yourself or others you may know are suffering.

Day 30 – The Lord's Prayer

The What

What we now refer to as The Lord's Prayer was intended as a model prayer for every Christian. The model teaches you many things about prayer and how you are to approach your God and heavenly Father. So what really is prayer?

- ✠ Prayer is an intimate conversation between you and God.
- ✠ Prayer provides you access to God at any time, at any place and for any reason. God is available 24 x 7 to you.
- ✠ Prayer is the time for you to have that "one-on-one" personal relationship with your heavenly Father. Prayer needs to come from the heart, not for the benefit of other people. (See Matthew 6:6.)
- ✠ Prayer is a gift and privilege that God has given to you.
- ✠ Prayer is meditation on God's Word and listening for His guidance and answers. Prayer is a two-way conversation. God speaks to you in prayer as well as through His Word. If you want answers to your prayers, be willing to listen – not just talk.

So how does The Lord's Prayer relate to God's attributes and to truly knowing God? Prior to giving the model prayer, Jesus tells us in Matthew 6:6-8 that God "sees what is done in secret" and "your

Father knows what you need before you ask him." In these statements Jesus is characterizing the Father as *omniscient, omnipresent and infinite*. It also means that God is *good* and cares for you as an individual. Your Father will hear and reward your prayers, because He is *faithful*. Prayer demonstrates the *personal* nature of God's relationship to you. Now let's break the prayer down and see what it tells us about God:

"Our Father in heaven"	Approach God as your Daddy (*Abba*) – versus the Old Testament belief where a person would not even call out the name Jehovah out of fear. Jesus has established a new relationship between God the Father and you - a personal relationship. This is your sonship with the *Father*; and expresses your love for the Father.
"hallowed be your name"	Go to God in reverence and acknowledge His *holiness*. Holy is your name must always be in your mind. You must always approach God with the thought that you are approaching the *holy* God Jehovah.
"your kingdom come"	recognize His *omnipotence and eternal* nature
"your will be done on earth as it is in heaven"	Acknowledge dependence on Him as well as His *sovereignty*, and acknowledge His perfect, yet permissive will. Ask for help in understanding His will for you.
"Give us today our daily bread"	Recognize that out of His *goodness* He is your provider and that He has promised to meet your needs daily. Daily dependence on God tests your faith in God's *faithfulness*.

"Forgive us our debts as we also have forgiven our debtors"

You must truly repent. Acknowledge your sin and God's promise to forgive your sins (His ***honesty and faithfulness***) but also acknowledge that your forgiveness is based on your responsibility to forgive others (See Matthew 6:14-15.). God wants you to be ***good, gracious and merciful*** to others just as He is to you. Forgiveness requires ***love and patience*** for others – just like God has for you. God wants you to imitate Him – be Christ-like.

"And lead us not into temptation"

Jesus was not saying that God tempts man or leads man into temptation. (See James 1:13.) The prayer is saying that we should not hesitate to petition God and ask Him to not allow us to suffer temptation. Asking, if it is within His will, to avoid temptation or suffering is not wrong. You should ask for protection from your weaknesses (human, earthly desires) – protection from yourself. Ask for the ***Holy Spirit*** to work in you and to make you holy and righteous.

"but deliver us from the evil one"

Ask God to rescue you when you fall short and protect you from the Devil.

So What?

It's good to have The Lord's Prayer as a model. It is also a good corporate prayer that can be prayed by many people together. However, too often when we say the Lord's Prayer, we repeat the words without any thought as to what we are saying. That is a recital, but not much of a prayer. God wants you to come to Him out of love and reverence, talking to Him from your heart. When you say The Lord's Prayer, really concentrate on each phrase and on God's attributes (as revealed in the prayer). This will help you draw closer to God. The Lord's Prayer should serve as an example for you in your personal prayers to God. Praise Him for all that He is in addition to taking your petitions to Him.

Selected Scripture
Matthew 6:5-15   Luke 11:1-13

Prayer
Pray the Lord's prayer and really focus on what the words mean. Whenever you need to pray and just can't get started because you do not know what to say, pray The Lord's Prayer and really think about all it means. Often this will lead to you saying what is in your heart.

Day 31 – Forgiveness

The What

Some might argue that we have left out one important attribute of God, which is forgiving. I have thought about this question, and have come to the conclusion that forgiveness is not an attribute of God like the others we have discussed. It is interesting that neither Tozer or Packer or Pink (three of the great theologians regarding God's nature) identified forgiving as an attribute of God. Why is this?

Let's examine several truths about God's forgiveness:

1. God's forgiveness is an action based on His *love, goodness, mercy and grace*. He forgives you because of who He is.
2. God's forgiveness is a reaction to you taking the initiative to confess your sins and truly repenting of them. He knows what is in your heart and mind.
3. God's forgiveness of our sins is dependent on how we forgive others. He knows what is in your heart and mind.
4. God's forgiveness is not based on your good works; God does not forgive you because you do some good things to make up for some bad things. If you truly want to re-connect with Him, get your heart right. He knows what is in your heart and mind.

On Day 30 we examined The Lord's Prayer. The part about forgiveness is the only part of the prayer that Jesus felt the need to explain. In Matthew 6:14-15 Jesus told us that if we forgive others, God will forgive us; but if we do not forgive others, God will not forgive us. I find it interesting that in the model prayer Jesus did not also say that He would, "Love us as we have also loved others." I'm speculating here, but I think it is because God is love 100% of the time; however, God is not forgiving 100% of the time. God is willing to forgive 100% of the time, but His forgiveness is dependent on us (see points 2-4 above).

In Matthew 18:21-35 Jesus explained the nature and dependency of God's forgiveness in the parable of the unmerciful servant. In those days the Rabbis taught to forgive someone three times. Peter, maybe desiring to look good to Jesus, asked if he should forgive someone up to seven times. Jesus' reply probably caught Peter off guard, because Jesus was basically saying don't keep track of how many times you forgive a brother. In the story of the unmerciful servant we can see the nature of God (represented by the king) in the king's response to the servant. The servant took the initiative to ask for forgiveness of his debt and sincerely said that he would try his best to pay back the debt. The king had pity – *compassion* - on the servant. He showed *mercy* by not punishing the servant and *grace* by totally canceling the debt. The king was *good*. The servant turned around and showed no compassion, mercy, or grace to a fellow servant who owed him a small debt. The servant was evil. There was no goodness in his heart. In verse 33, the king, after hearing what the wicked servant had done called the servant in and said, "Shouldn't you have had mercy on your fellow servant just as I had on you?" The king brings his wrath upon the evil servant and punishes him. Then in verse 35, Jesus makes it clear: **"This is how my heavenly Father will treat each of you unless you forgive your brother** *from your heart.***"**

If someone does you wrong and you cannot find it in your heart to forgive him, why would God punish you? After all, the other person is the one who did you wrong. Think about it this way: if you are unforgiving to someone else, then you are not truly confessing all of your sins and repenting, so how can you ask for forgiveness from God. There is hate, malice, and unforgiveness in your heart; and these are sins. Wickedness, not love, is in your heart. In 1 John 4:8 we are told: **"Whoever does not love does not know God, because God is love."**

So What?

Forgiveness goes against our human nature when we are walking in the flesh. When someone does wrong to you, you should get in step with the Holy Spirit. While it might be difficult or impossible for you to forgive someone, all things are possible with God. With the help of the Holy Spirit you can forgive. It is essential to forgive others so that hate and malice will not be in your heart.

Imitate Jesus Christ. His death on the cross was the perfect model for both love and forgiveness. He died for us out of love, and his death cancelled **all** our sin debts. In Matthew 18:33 Jesus is clearly telling us to imitate His mercy and forgiveness. Christ is not looking for payment for our sins; He wants repentance and a change of heart. When someone wrongs you and seeks forgiveness, cancel the debt or trespass completely – else you will always be looking for payment (or payback). That is the true Biblical meaning of forgiveness.

It may be counter-intuitive; but if you completely fill your heart with love, there will be room for forgiveness. But if you empty your heart of love, there will be no room for forgiveness.

"So in everything, do to others what you would have them do to you." (Matthew 7:12) Everything includes forgiveness.

Forgive others as you desire for God to forgive you.

Selected Scripture
Matthew 18:21-35; 6:14-15; 7:12   Ephesians 4:31-32
1 John 4:7-8

Prayer

Pray for strength and love to forgive another person that has done something bad to you.

Pray that evil thoughts, malice and hatred will be removed from your heart.

Day 32 – The Resurrection

The What

D r. Charles Stanley says, "Christ rose to validate and settle once and for all that our God is the only true God, the Creator of all things." (1) Paul tells us that without the resurrection of Jesus Christ, everything we have studied in this book and everything you believe in as a Christian would be in vain – without any foundation. The resurrection is awesome proof that our God lives. The resurrection is paramount to the Christian faith and therefore reveals many of God's attributes in a way no other act by God could. Let's examine some of these:

Attribute	How the Resurrection Revealed
The Holy Trinity	The resurrection is the "acid test" for the divinity of Jesus Christ. Scripture tells us that at the resurrection of Jesus all three persons of the Trinity acted in unity for the purpose and will of God.
Infinite, Divine	Only the true, infinite, divine God could unveil a plan hundreds of years in advance, ensure the plan came to fruition, and then have power over death – something no created being could possibly do.

Eternal	The resurrection is clear evidence of God's eternity. Death holds no power over our God.
Unchanging	God has always been holy, loving, merciful, gracious, omnipotent, sovereign, just and jealous. God determined a perfect plan for man's salvation and never altered His plan.
Glorious, Majestic	Perhaps in no other way have God's glory and majesty been revealed on earth as magnificently as in Jesus' resurrection, appearance and ascension.
Omniscient, Wise	Old Testament prophets as well as Jesus prophesized that He (Jesus) would be killed, buried and resurrected. The resurrection is the culmination of God's wise and perfect plan for man's salvation and reconciliation to Him.
Omnipotent	The resurrection demonstrates God's power over death. The resurrection also gave evidence of God's power over His physical creation (rolling back of the stone, sudden appearances of a physical body).
Faithful, Honest and Trustworthy	God's forgiveness of our sins and our eternal life are foundational promises of God. The resurrection of Jesus is our assurance of the fulfillment of that promise. It also gives us evidence that we will be resurrected as well.
Good and Compassionate	The goodness of God through the resurrection provides each of us with the ability to live life more abundantly here on earth and eternally in heaven. We can have peace and assurance through the resurrection that God forgives us, loves us, and wants us to spend an eternity in heaven with Him. We can feel

	confident it is not by something we have to earn, but by God's gift, that we are saved.
Just	God views Christ's substitutionary death as a just payment, or penalty, for our sins. This provides justice while allowing God's gift of love and grace.
Merciful, Gracious And Love	The death and resurrection of Jesus was the perfect demonstration and culmination of God's love, mercy and grace. He paid the price!
Worthy	The resurrection demonstrates God's worthiness to us on a personal level.
Jealous	The resurrection shows us that faith in Jesus is *the* way, *the* truth and *the* life. He is a jealous God and demands our faith in Him and His promises, not in something concocted by man.
Holy, Righteous	Jesus lived a holy, righteous, sin-free life so that He would be the acceptable sacrifice, the last necessary sacrifice for our sins.
Sovereign	Jesus' resurrection showed God's sovereignty over the greatest earthly rulers and religious leaders and over all spiritual powers. He had a plan and His plan could not be thwarted by Satan or Roman and Jewish authorities. Jesus said He had the authority to lay down His life and to raise it up again.
Father	Believers in the Christ are God's forgiven, loved children – co-heirs with Christ of God's kingdom.

So What?

Because of the Resurrection, you can have confidence and assurance in knowing:

-   Your God lives.

- Your sins are forgiven, and you will have an eternal life in heaven. There is no reason to fear death.
- Since Christ lives, God is actively involved in your life. (2)

Know that in Christ, you have a proven Savior. Again Dr. Stanley states, "The Resurrection earned and deserves our trust for all that Christ ever claimed, promised, warned, or predicted." (3)

If you would like to read more about Resurrection evidence, read Part 3 of Lee Strobel's book, <u>The Case for Christ</u>.

Selected Scripture
John 11:25-26   John 3:16-17   Romans 5:8 John 10:17-18
1 Corinthians 15:1-34 Philippians 3:7-11

Prayer
Thank God for our Savior who has risen and lives.
Praise Him for clearly revealing His power and glory in Jesus' resurrection.
Thank Him for providing enough evidence to encourage our faith and hope.

Day 33 – Heaven and Hell

The What

Heaven and hell force us to think about God. Often this results in many arguments about the nature of God and whether heaven and hell actually exist. Often people think about a god with two personalities. One is totally good, loving and gracious. The other is angry, jealous and wrathful. However, in this book we are trying to get you to see how God is who He is – 100% of His attributes, 100% percent of the time. He does not turn attributes on and off. Instead they work in complete harmony to the fulfillment of His will. Heaven and hell are discussed throughout the Bible and are a foundational promise of God. Let's examine how all of God's attributes work together in complete harmony when we examine the justice of heaven and hell.

- God is *holy*, so God detests sin. In Habakkuk 1:13 we find these pointed words: **"Your (God's) eyes are too pure to look on evil; you cannot tolerate wrong."**
- God is *immutable*, so He will always hate sin.
- God is a *just* God, and His *justice* is seen in both salvation and in judgment. Neither a saved person nor a condemned person will experience injustice at the hands of Almighty God. There will be no favorites – just fairness.

- God is *self-sufficient,* that is, He does not need you or me. Our presence in heaven is not required for God to continue existing.
- God is *faithful.* He has promised both heaven and hell, so they both will happen. God has promised He will forgive your sins if you repent; and He has promised you life eternal in heaven. Again I repeat that He is a *faithful* God; so you can count 100% on His promises.
- God is the *creator* of both heaven and hell.
- Heaven is a holy place, and nothing unholy will enter there. That would rule out you, me and everyone else. Thankfully God's *love* for you is infinite and unconditional and eternal; and His *goodness* drives Him to want what is best for you. Hence, God has prepared a holy heaven with a plan for *eternal* salvation for you. His *goodness* drives this salvation plan to be a gift from Him, through His *grace*. His *love* drives Him to make the payment for the gift.
- God's *mercy* spares you punishment for disobedience and sin – if you accept His gift of salvation.
- God self-imposes a limitation on His *omniscience*, as He not only forgives, but forgets your sins. When He forgives you, He no longer sees a sinful person.
- God is *jealous* so he will punish the unrighteous that reject or ignore Him. The most important thing to God is our relationship to Him, not how good or bad we are. Remember the motives for His jealousy are pure; because He loves you, and He desires what is best for you – an *eternity* in heaven with Him. However, if you choose not to have a relationship with God, He will grant you your wish for *eternity*.
- God is *omnipotent* and *sovereign* over His creation, so He can and will make all of this happen.
- God is also a *creative* God. Although in 1 Corinthians 2:9 it says that man cannot even conceive how wonderful heaven will be, that verse concludes with **"but God has revealed it to us by His Spirit."** God has given us enough information in His Word about heaven that we should long for it – if we know and trust Him. Think about God's *creativity*,

and imagine how unbelievably wonderful this earth would be without sin and natural disasters. Think about how rich we all would be without murder, theft, cheating, malicious behavior, coveting, etc. What if everyone wanted what was best for everyone else? What if we were all true friends?

= No locks on doors.	= No fear of other people.
= No war.	= No need for police.
= People helping each other.	= People sharing with each other.
= The beauty of nature.	= The freedom to travel and explore.

Even if death was still a reality, this would be quite a world. Well, if I can imagine that, I can't wait to see the eternal treasures that I <u>cannot</u> even fathom.

So What?

Make a choice. If you do not know exactly where you stand, make the effort to know where you stand – either with Christ or against Him. As Joshua pleaded, **"choose for yourselves this day whom you will serve." (Joshua 24:15)** Refer to Appendix E – Choice.

Take time to dwell on heaven. Don't let the distractions of this world keep you from spending a little time each day reflecting on eternal matters and promises. Set your heart on things above. Be confident in God's promises and look forward to heaven with anticipation.

Do not be misled by today's spiritual doubletalk or by the "spiritualism de jour". The commonly accepted spiritual belief today is universalism – all religions are good and lead to God. This sounds good because it is easy and does not offend. However, it simply is not Biblical; and it takes away the meaning of and message of Jesus Christ. If hell is not real, then Jesus lied. (In the Gospels Jesus talked about hell over 50 times.)

Hell may be a terrifying thought, but you need fear it only if you are not saved. However, be concerned for unsaved friends and family and strangers. Use hell, as well as God's heaven, as a springboard to witnessing.

Selected Scripture

Ephesians 2:4-9	John 3:16; 14:1-4	1 Corinthians 2:9
Colossians 3:1-4	1 John 5:13	
2 Thessalonians 1:8-10	Hebrews 10:29-31	2 Peter 3:9

Prayer

Thank God for his promises of heaven.

Pray that you will not be distracted by life's worries or pleasures.

Pray for the Holy Spirit to reveal truths that will instill you to take action for your salvation or for the salvation of others.

Pray for unsaved friends and family. Be specific in your prayers.

Day 34 – As Seen in Jesus

John 14:7	Jesus said, **"If you really knew me you would know my Father as well. From now on, you do know him and have seen him."**
Hebrews 1:3	**"The Son is the radiance of God's glory and the exact representation of his being…"**
Colossians 1:19	**"For God was pleased to have all his fullness dwell in him."**
Colossians 2:9	**"For in Christ all the fullness of the Deity lives in bodily form."**
Colossians 1:15	**"He is the image of the invisible God, the firstborn over all creation."**
Philippians 2:6	**"Who, being in the very nature of God …"**

The What

Have you ever wondered why God took on the form of man to come and dwell on earth as Jesus Christ? Take a minute to ponder that question in your mind. Knowing the answer to this question is important for your own faith and for your witness.

My answer is one word: LOVE. I believe God created man for His glory and because of His desire for mutual love. God loves man because of who He is; God has given man the choice to love Him in return. God could have created a being that had no free will and would have obeyed every command without exception; but I believe this being would have had an empty heart – robotic in nature. Instead, God chose to create man in His image with free will and the ability to make choices. Think about it; only an absolutely sovereign God could yield some control into the hands of His created beings. Reflect on the major choices we can make that pertain to our direct relationship with our Creator God:

1. Whether to believe God exists
2. Whether to believe in the true God (or which god to believe in)
3. Daily choices between holy and evil, good and bad, right and wrong
4. Whether to trust God or trust in someone (or something) else
5. Whether to love, worship, serve, obey and share God or to ignore God
6. Whether to have a personal relationship with God

Again, these are my heartfelt beliefs; but I believe Jesus Christ was a very logical way for God to do what He wanted to do. To me, it is the perfect plan. But it is the perfect plan because it is God's plan, not because I think it is. Let's think about it using the logical minds God has given to us.

Let's look at a few facts real quickly:

1. God is holy and detests sin.
2. God created a magnificent universe for His glory.
3. God desired that a special part of His creation (mankind) should have free will. This free will allows man to choose to come to Him out of love, faith, trust, respect and worship, fear, or not to come to Him at all. Free will also allows mankind to make choices between good and evil.
4. God, in His omniscience, knew that man would sin and that sin would separate man from God.
5. God, in His infinite wisdom and divine purpose, provides the perfect, logical solution (Jesus Christ) to reconcile man to

Him – to heal or bridge this separation. Jesus lived a sinless, *holy, righteous* life because of whom He was, God incarnate, 100% God and 100% human. God gave us the *perfect* atoning sacrifice for the sins of mankind, because He was man yet He was without the blemish of sin. However, God still requires each person to still make the decision to trust Him and accept His plan of salvation.

6.   God reveals this plan to mankind in such a way that it can be clearly understood, but still requires man to seek God and come to Him out of faith.

Belief in Jesus requires the ultimate in our belief, faith and trust in God and His will. We cannot devise our own plan; we cannot devise a better plan; and we cannot come to God except by God's Way. We are *dependent on God* alone. That brings glory to God.

Think back to Day 3 to the logical problems of trying to earn your way into God's good grace and into heaven. With every other religion or way of thinking about God, there is uncertainty, doubt and lack of hope. Jesus Christ eliminates these unsolvable problems. In one of my favorite verses we can understand the freedom that Christ talked about when He said that the truth will set you free:

Ephesians 3:12 "In him and through faith in him we may approach God with freedom and confidence."

Isn't it great to know that the one, true, Almighty God gives you the Way to stand before Him with total freedom and confidence knowing that He loves you! You can be free from worrying about whether you have earned your way to heaven or been good enough in God's eyes. You can be assured of your salvation. Understand that this view of God's nature is unique to Christianity.

God's plan of salvation is a perfect, freedom-giving, loving and gracious gift. In Jesus, God demonstrates His *love* for man by sharing first hand with His creation. He provides the perfect and just way by which a *Holy* God can have a relationship with unholy beings, and still allow them the freedom to choose how to live their lives. Jesus is the means by which you can have a personal relationship to God the Father. Everything about Jesus is because of God's love for you His child – His birth, His life, His death, and His resurrection.

God's love for you is the reason for Jesus coming to this earth!

<u>*So What?*</u>
So what should this mean to you? Jesus Christ is proof positive that God loves and <u>values</u> you. In Luke 15, Jesus tells in the parables of the lost sheep and the lost coin how much God values us. Jesus Christ is God actively seeking you – His child. Even though you are one person among billions, understand that God loves you and places value on your life and spirit. What a thought! You, *(your name)*, are important to God!

This may seem obvious, but I have to state it - believing in the Deity of Christ is what makes a Christian a Christian. If all you can say is that "Yea, I believe in God"; but in your heart you do not believe in Jesus Christ as His Son, then you do not truly know the true God. Once you have come to grasp the Trinity as well as the Divinity of Christ, you will better understand God's plan of salvation for man. The fact that salvation is by God's grace and not by your works is predicated on the incarnation of Christ. Other religions believe in a god without the divinity of Jesus. Once you see Jesus as God, then you can see God in His person, actions and teachings; and you can see how grace, compassion and mercy flow out of His love for you.

Honor God by depending on Him and trusting Him. Through Jesus, God has reached out His hand to you. Choose to grasp it and hold on tight for an eternal thrill ride.

<u>*Selected Scripture*</u>
Luke 15:1-10; 19:10   John 3:16-17

<u>*Prayer*</u>
Thank God for the gift of Jesus Christ and for loving us so much as to descend to become like man.

Praise Jesus for being our Good Shepherd who was willing to die for His sheep.

Thank God for such a clear and meaningful revelation of Himself.

Note: You can refer to Appendix C for a detailed list of Scripture that identifies specifically how Jesus manifested each of the divine attributes of God.

How Can You Apply Your Knowledge of God's Attributes in Daily Living?

Day 35 - Reflecting God's Image

The What

I t is said that imitation is purest form of flattery. When you as a Christian truly strive to imitate Christ, it is the purest form of honor that you can give God. I believe that is truly what makes God smile.

My Bible Study class got into a debate over the question: "When are we most human – when we are sinning or when we are obedient and holy?" One point of view was that it is human nature to satisfy yourself and to commit sin. When a person does something wrong and responds with the excuse "well, after all, I am only human", they are saying that it is human nature to sin. The opposing view was that man is made in the image of God and is, therefore, more human when being obedient to God and living holy. After thinking about this question, I believe both sides are right. Man is made in the image of God and has a spirit – but man also has a mind and a body. If a person is not saved, he is living in the flesh and his mind is focused on earthly things; and it is most human to sin. We all have a sin nature. But if we have been born again into God's family, God's Holy Spirit will abide within us. If we truly love God, we will obey God. Our spirit will walk in step with the Holy Spirit. More and more, our spirit will control our mind and we will focus on eternal, spiritual, heavenly things. Children of God are humans that try to be more Christ-like and try to take on God's attributes of love, grace, mercy, faithfulness, etc. It is most human for a child of God to strive to be obedient and live a holy life.

You have spent several weeks getting to know God by learning about His attributes. You also know that you are made in the image of God. Colossians 3:9-10 states where you should be right now: **"since you have taken off your old self with its practices and have put on the new self, which is being renewed in knowledge in the image of its Creator."** So how should your life, thoughts and actions reflect your proper knowledge and understanding of God? Paul says you should **"shine like stars in the universe"** (Philippians 2:15) and **"Be imitators of God"**. (Ephesians 5:1) Remember at the front of this booklet we stated that one of our goals was to stimulate you to be more Christ-like in your character. You now have the knowledge of God's image so that you can shine like the stars.

Becoming more Christ-like should be the goal of every true Christian. This is a lifelong journey or process, not an occasional step. The Bible has much to say about what your character and behavior should be if you are a true child of God. There are certain qualities that you should exhibit so that other people will recognize you as a Christian. The key ones are:

Galatians 5:22-26	love, joy, peace, patience, kindness, goodness, faithfulness, gentleness, and self-control
2 Peter 1:5-8	goodness, knowledge, self-control, perseverance, godliness, brotherly kindness, love
James 3:17-18	wisdom, pure, peace-loving, considerate, submissive, full of mercy and good fruit, impartial, sincere, and righteous
Col. 3:12-17	holy, compassion, kindness, humility, gentleness, patience, forgiving (mercy), love, wisdom, gratefulness

Jesus Christ and the Word of God specifically focus on two qualities of every follower: love and forgiveness. In Ephesians 4:32

God has commanded us to forgive one another, just as Christ has forgiven you. And in John 15:12 Jesus states: **"My command is this: Love each other as I have loved you."** With these two qualities, God commands you to be perfect imitators.

So What?
Make God smile. Be an imitator of Christ.

Make being Christ-like your lifelong goal. Know that you will fall short. When you sin, do not let the sin become a habit. Do not allow the sin to trouble you with guilt. Repent of it and get back on track towards your goal.

Be very conscious of your thoughts and actions knowing that they will either reflect the devil or they will reflect Christ. Christ was our example. Likewise, you should be the example to the rest of the world. Be a light unto the world.

The process of becoming more Christ-like is not a battle you have to fight alone. That is one of the very reasons for the gift and in-dwelling of the Holy Spirit. The Holy Spirit will strengthen and guide you in your daily life. However, you must seek His help and yield to His will, or as Paul says, walk in step with the Spirit.

Selected Scripture
Matthew 12:33-37   John 13:34-35   1 John 4:11-12
Ephesians 5:1-2

Prayer
Ask God for the power of the Holy Spirit to help you fight your battles.
Ask for the Spirit's guidance in your daily affairs.
Repent of your sins soon after you recognize them.

Day 36 – In Obedience

The What

When you consider obedience, serving, witnessing and worshipping, which of these do you think is most important and why? I am going to propose that obedience is the most important to you as a believer because of these for four reasons:

1. Scripture clearly states that if you love God, you will obey His commands. (See John 14:15, 23-24; 1 John 5:2-3.) Obedience demonstrates your love for God.
2. To remain in God's love, you must obey His commands. (See John 15:9-10.) You will be God's friend if you obey His commands. (See John 15:14.)
3. Disobedience is sin and creates a chasm, or separation, between you and God. Obedience will draw you nearer to God.
4. You cannot <u>effectively</u> serve the Lord, witness for the Lord, or worship the Lord unless you are first obedient.

Webster defines obedience as being submissive to the commands of authority. As Christians our authority is God, but the question is: what do we see as His commands? We could take a narrow view and say, for example, that the Ten Commandments, revealed by God the Father, are His commands. We could add God the Son's

(Jesus) statement about the two greatest commandments being: (1) loving God with all your heart, soul and mind and (2) loving your neighbors as yourself. We could add all the specific commands in New Testament Scripture about forgiveness, witnessing, worship, judging others, etc. Scripture identifies many specific do's and don'ts by which we should live our lives. However, I believe that we need to apply the broadest definition of obedience to our lives, an obedience that comes from deep within us – when God's commands are written on our hearts. It is accurate to say that obedience to God is reflected in your **conduct**, which means doing good things and not doing bad things, as defined in Scripture. The broader definition of obedience to God, however, is also following His will in our lives. This can only be done when His commands are upon our hearts and the Holy Spirit works within us and guides us in our daily activities and choices. This broader definition of obedience to God will be reflected in our **character, contemplations and conversation**, which all reflect our hearts and souls. (1)

Studying God's Word, praying, worshipping and obedience all result in more fullness of the Holy Spirit. Likewise, more fullness of the Holy Spirit makes obedience easier and more natural. Picture a window air conditioning unit that is installed in the den of a five-room house. The unit is more than adequate to cool the whole house. However, if the bedroom and bathroom doors are shut, they will not be cooled. The cool air is shut out of these rooms. Having the fullness of the Holy Spirit at work in a person's life is analogous to this air-conditioned house. If the person shuts the Holy Spirit out of parts of his/her life (at school, at work, Friday nights, etc.), that person cannot experience the fullness of the Holy Spirit. To this person, obedience is part-time and optional based on his/her circumstances. Disobedience becomes easier and justifiable in this person's mind. However, when someone opens the "rooms" of his/her life, the Holy Spirit begins to fill the person more and more; and obedience becomes something the person desires to do – not something he/she has to do.

A person can obey God out of fear of the consequences of disobedience. There is nothing wrong with that. However, as a person matures in Christ and his/her knowledge of God increases, that person's passion to obey God will evolve and grow. The person will choose to obey God, simply because HE IS WHO HE IS - awesome, eternal, infinite, loving, gracious, omnipotent, sovereign, etc. He is worthy of obedience. If your passion for Christ reaches this level, you will truly want to obey Him, because you love Him. You will view Him as worthy of your respect, and obedience shows respect. Your knowledge and intimacy with the Holy One will fuel your passion to obey Him.

So What?

Obedience to God can demonstrate your love and respect for God. You can honor and glorify God through your obedience; because, through your acts of obedience, you are telling God and all other people that "He is my God".

Make a commitment to God to obey Him in your conduct, character, contemplations and conversation. Make obedience from your heart a goal. Make obedience the bottom-line in your decision-making, and commit to obedience regardless of the consequences.

Study God's Word so that His commands are deeply rooted within your mind. Seek the revelation and guidance of the Holy Spirit to help you discern right from wrong and how to apply God's Word to specific circumstances that you face in your life. Let your conscience be your guide, and let the Holy Spirit guide your conscience. Make obedience to God more important to you than the opinions of others.

Do not set limitations on how much you are going to obey God. Dr. Charles Stanley says that when you start saying things like: "I can obey except for...." or "I will obey Him, but if ..." or "I can obey Him except when...", then you ***cannot*** call Christ Lord of your life. (2) You are setting conditions on when you will obey God, which is essentially saying He is your part-time Lord.

Do not attempt to rationalize disobedience. When you choose to disobey, you are saying that you are wise enough to make the determination as to when it is okay. Do not use God's mercy and grace and willingness to forgive as a convenient excuse to disobey.

Use God's grace and mercy as a motivation to holy living (obedience), not as a license to sin (disobedience).

Remember God knows your heart.

Selected Scripture
John 14:15, 23-26, 15:9-14   James 1:22-25   1 John 3:6, 5:2-3
Matthew 28:20

Prayer
Pray for the fullness of the Holy Spirit and for His guidance in all matters of your life.
Immediately repent and ask for forgiveness when you are disobedient.
Pray for strength in areas where you are weak.

Day 37 – In Serving

The What

As a new set of episodes begins on the TV show "The Apprentice", Donald Trump walks into the room and meets the twelve people trying out for the apprenticeship. After a few minutes of introductions and discussion, Mr. Trump gets out of his chair, takes off his coat and walks over to the corner of the room. Without saying a word, he picks up a box and removes a brush, some polish, and some cloths. He then goes to one of the wannabes, kneels down, and begins to shine that person's shoes. He proceeds around the room doing the same to each person. One of the contestants tells Mr. Trump that he will not let his boss belittle and humble himself by shining his shoes; however, Trump tells him that he will be fired immediately if he does not allow him to do this. After finishing with the twelve persons, he tells them that he has done this to demonstrate that if they want to succeed in his business they must learn to serve and help others. What is going on here? Well, obviously it is a huge figment of my imagination. It would never happen! Not in a hundred or a thousand years. The show is about one-upping the others, egos, looking out for number one, etc.

Something similar did happen 2,000 years ago in the upper room of a house in Jerusalem. The person, however, was infinitely more important, glorious and worthy than Mr. Trump. (I do not mean this as a slap at Donald Trump.) In John 13:1-17 we are told Jesus washed the feet of His disciples. He did this for two reasons. First Jesus wanted to illustrate that we would all need periodic cleansing of our sins, but only for the parts that are dirty; because the body of a Christian is already clean. Second, he also washed their feet to demonstrate how we are to humble ourselves and serve one another. Pride, status, and egos have no place in the kingdom of God.

In Isaiah 52:13 the prophecy about the coming Messiah refers to Jesus Christ as God's servant. **"See, my servant will act wisely; he will be raised and lifted up and highly exalted."** Jesus, the man, was God's servant because He did God's will on earth. Jesus was our model servant. His service was based on God's love for us – just as our service should be based on our love for God and our love for others.

Many of Jesus' parables demonstrated the importance Christ placed on service. In Luke 10:25-37 we read about one of the most famous, the parable of The Good Samaritan. This parable demonstrates how we can serve God through the spiritual gift of showing mercy and compassion. Some people are more gifted than others when it comes to serving in this way; but, in this example, we are all called to serve others, regardless of our status or the status or the race of the person needing help. We should not be concerned about who is watching or not watching or if we will be recognized for our good deed. The deed should be done to honor God, to show our love for Him, to obey Him and because we love others. We are all called to serve God.

Service truly affords each of us the opportunity to reflect God's image and to be Christ-like in our lives. *Love, mercy, grace, compassion, patience, abundant goodness, and faithfulness* are all attributes that we can take on and demonstrate in service to God and others. These characteristics are how you will be known as a disciple of Christ.

Serving and helping others is a way to be a witness for Christ without having to say a word. Sometimes actions do speak louder than words. If others see these attributes in you, they will think that you know your God and believe your God is *worthy* of your time, energy, and service. You plant a seed that may one day grow.

So What?

Make a strong, genuine effort to determine your spiritual gift(s). Work with you church leadership to determine how you can help the church and serve God through your gifts and talents.

Do not waste the talents and time the Lord has given you. You will be held accountable for your works. I heard Pastor Adrian Rogers once say, "You are not saved by your works, but are saved by a faith that works."

Do not let pride or laziness get in the way. Fight to overcome any obstacles that prevent you from serving as you should.

On the day you stand before God Almighty what could be a better reward than to hear your Father say, "Well done, good and faithful servant."

Selected Scripture

John 13:1-17   Luke 10:25-37   James 2:14-26
Matthew 20:26-28

Prayer

If you have avoided serving the Lord, pray for help in identifying opportunities for service. Make a commitment to God that you will serve.
Pray that you may find ways to help encourage others to serve.
Pray that your service will bring glory and honor to God.

Day 38 – In Witnessing

The What

Webster defines a "witness" as a person who:

1. Gives evidence, and
2. Has personal knowledge of something

A Christian witness provides evidence and argument for the personal knowledge he/she has of God the Father and Jesus Christ. Truly knowing God is the key. First, knowledge *about* the true God gives your testimony substance, validity and accuracy. Second, personal knowledge *of* God, based on a personal relationship with Him, creates passion within you and credibility with the person to whom you are witnessing. Third, knowing God also means that you can reflect God's attributes and be Christ-like in your witness. Let's look at an example of what we are talking about so that you can see what being an effective witness for Christ requires.

Let's look at John 4:1-42 where Jesus meets and testifies to the Samaritan woman at the well where she is simply going about her daily activities. Jesus, being the exact representation of God, gives us a good example of how to witness to a stranger.

1. Jesus was ***good*** to the woman and genuinely concerned for her welfare.

2. He was *omniscient*, knowing the details of her past.
3. Jesus was *righteous and holy*, addressing her sinfulness.
4. Jesus was *wise* in how He drew her to Himself.
5. He was *merciful* and *compassionate* in that He did not reject her for her status or past.
6. He was *just* and not judgmental, not allowing others to affect how He dealt with her. He gave her a chance to put her past behind her.
7. Jesus *patiently* answered her questions.
8. Jesus was *faithful* to the promises of God and *lovingly* forgave her sins. (1)

Jesus powerfully reflects God's attributes in this story. Now, you cannot reflect God's attribute of omniscience, but you can show genuine concern by listening and trying to understand a person's problems and questions. Be as Christ-like as possible, and you will be a more effective witness.

In the story we also see the power of an effective witness. Jesus simply planted the seed, and things began to happen. The woman immediately turns around and becomes an effective witness. The power of multiplication takes over and soon many others come to know Jesus. But how could the testimony of a woman, a sinful woman, at the bottom of the social ladder, become so effective, so quickly? From the story we can tell the woman knew some things about God. She knew Scripture and she knew about a coming Messiah; but she did not yet truly know God. There, by the well, she truly came to know of God through Jesus. She could see a *merciful, loving* God who would be her Savior and a burning passion was ignited within the woman.

Know the God for whom you witnessing.
Experience the God for whom you are witnessing.
Reflect the God for whom you are witnessing.

So What?
Witnessing will be the clearest indication of the strength and conviction of your faith in God and your relationship with Him,

because you are putting your faith on the line in front of others. If you are not sure of what you believe, if you have reservations or doubts, if your faith is not solid, if your only knowledge of God is inaccurate or very cursory, then the person will see through you. The Holy Spirit must be working inside of you, else simple questions and issues will confound you. So how can you be an effective witness?

1. Develop your personal relationship with God in order to fuel a burning passion to witness, serve, obey, and worship.
2. Be prepared to share the hope that is within you (1 Peter 3:15-16). You can do this by developing your knowledge about God through reading the Scripture and studying other materials. Understand God's attributes and how they work together in His plan of salvation. However, it takes more than just facts. You also need to know why you believe and be prepared to put this into words. Write down your testimony and the basis of your faith and rehearse it in your mind. Also be prepared to answer some of the common questions that people have. Many of these can be addressed through knowledge of God's attributes.
3. Pray for the help of the Holy Spirit. You simply cannot be effective without His counsel and revelation.
4. Make a commitment to witness and serve Jesus. Witnessing for Jesus Christ is one form of serving Him. On the flip side, there are many ways to witness for Jesus Christ; and serving Jesus Christ, in any manner, is a form of witnessing for Him. Your actions can result in your being an effective witness for Christ and will give you opportunities to informally share Christ with others.
5. Take the first step and do it. Look for an opportunity and seize it.
6. Be Christ-like in your witnessing. Do not be arrogant, condescending, judgmental, impatient, and uncaring. Show the person that the love of Christ lives in you.
7. Do not get turned off if the person does not respond to your witness. You have planted a seed. You have obeyed Christ.

He commanded you to witness, not to save. That is the work of the Holy Spirit.

Maybe all of this can best be summed up in a great song called: "I Want People to See Jesus in Me". If people cannot see Jesus in you, then you cannot witness to them. If they can see Jesus in you, then verbal witnessing becomes easier.

Selected Scripture
John 4:1-42   1 Peter 3:15-16

Prayer
Pray for the Holy Spirit to help you and prepare you to be an effective witness. When an opportunity to witness occurs, quickly pray for the power of the Holy Spirit to help you and to touch the heart of the person to whom you are witnessing.

Day 39 – In Worshipping

The What

A life of worship is the culmination of taking the knowledge we have studied about God and applying it to our personal relationship with God. On Day 36 I proposed that obedience is most important to you as a believer because you cannot effectively serve, witness or worship unless you are trying to live a righteous life. However, proper worship is the most important thing we can do in our relationship with God. Worship is all about God, and not about us. Think about it, I can serve God even if I just feel I need to do something "to do my part". I can pray out of hope and despair or for God to meet my needs. I can obey out of fear or even just to look good to others. However, I cannot genuinely worship without it being about Him.

Take a couple of minutes to study John 4:19-24 (or if time permits John 4:4-24). In this story Jesus meets the Samaritan woman by the well and engages her in a conversation. "Jesus used the word "worship" or "worshiper" seven times in his conversation with the Samaritan woman. He made it clear that worship isn't about place. It doesn't happen simply because we know the right things about God. Rather, worship flows from spirit and truth – from knowing God himself." (1) In John 4:23 Jesus tells us that **"true worshipers will worship in spirit and truth, for they are the kind of worshipers the Father seeks."** God desires and seeks true worshipers. In John

4:24 Jesus gives us a specific commandment when He says, **"God is spirit, and his worshipers must worship in spirit and in truth."** The meaning of this verse does not exactly leap off the page at you. It requires some careful thought.

First, the root of the Hebrew word translated "worship" means "to bow down". Worship is "the soul bowing before God in adoring contemplation of Him." (2) To worship in spirit means that we worship by the Spirit of God. We need to seek the help of the Holy Spirit so that our thoughts and energy are focused on God and not on the concerns of our flesh. Our focus is on the praise, adoration and worship of God for who He is. We humble ourselves and lift up God in true worship. To worship in truth means that we must know the truth, and the truth comes from the Word of God and from God the Holy Spirit who reveals the truth to us. Hopefully this study has helped you to know God better and to draw closer in your relationship with Him. In Rick Warren's book <u>The Purpose Driven Life</u>, he lists four characteristics about worship that please God. The first one is that: "God is pleased when our worship is accurate."(3) God desires that we worship Him for whom He is, not whom we would like for our god to be. By studying His attributes, you should have an accurate understanding of God and can better worship Him in truth. Dr. Charles Stanley says, "When you praise Him for His attributes, you put your attention on His worthiness, and that's the very purpose of your worship."(4)

In John 12:1-8 we see one of the simplest, purest forms of worship. Mary takes a pint of pure nard, an expensive perfume, and pours it on Jesus' feet and wipes His feet with her hair. Mary is truly worshipping Jesus. This "was a pure expression of the love and worship in Mary's heart." (5) She <u>truly knew</u> Jesus and felt He was worthy of her worship. She did not concern herself with what others thought. She humbled herself. She wanted to give Jesus something of value. She wanted Jesus to know how much she adored Him. And the real kicker is that this brought joy to Jesus!

So What?

If you consider God worthy of your worship and praise, then:

1. Take the time to worship and praise Him. Put Him at the top of your list of priorities, not as a secondary thought.
2. Humble yourself before God. God is real; God is awesome; God is glorious; and God is worthy.
3. Worship God in spirit. This requires your deep love and reverence. This is worship from your heart. Seek the help of the Holy Spirit to properly worship.
4. Worship God in truth and mind. This requires you to completely devote your thoughts and energy to your worship. This also requires you to worship Him accurately based on who He is. Remember – HE IS WHO HE IS. Strive to know Him.

If you truly know God and if you truly love God, worshipping Him should be easy, natural and joyous. If you see worship as a burden because it imposes on your time, then you need to take stock of your relationship with God. If you cannot surrender to Him or humble yourself before Him without reservation, then perhaps you cannot say He is Lord of your life.

Remember worship is not just attending church services and dutifully performing the religious rituals at a service. We are talking about truly worshipping God – whether in church or daily in your mind regardless of where you are – because you want to worship Him. Consider it an honor to be able to worship Him.

Ravi Zacharias states that true worship is about holiness, not happiness. Too often in our "worship" we want to be entertained. We consider ourselves to be part of an audience; but, in true worship, God is the audience.

God is all of the attributes we have studied. Take time to truly know Him. Then you will know that He is absolutely worthy of all of your praise and worship. This awesome God of the universe loves you, (*insert your name*), and He knows you, too. Shouldn't you, shouldn't we all, be absolutely overjoyed to worship Him?

Selected Scripture
John 4:19-24; 12:1-8   Psalm 68:4   Psalm 100
Hebrews 12:28-29

Prayer

Meditate on God's attributes and pick a few that perhaps, because of some circumstances in your life, are special to you at this time. Praise Him for who He is.

Express your love, adoration and respect for your God. Make God smile.

Day 40 - Self Analysis

The What

Well, here we are at the last day of this study. We hope that you now know more about God than you did before the study and have taken this opportunity to truly know God on a personal, intimate level. Now is a good time to find out just how well you know God. We are not going to ask you to list and define all the attributes of God. That would give you a good indication of what you know *about* God. Instead, we are going to ask you a simple question that is probably as good an indication of how well you know God as anything else we could ask. The question is this:

To you personally, how worthy is God?

Let's take a minute to reflect on what we have studied and meditated on during the last 40 days. Let your imagination run wild, and you still will not be able to grasp how awesome God is, but consider some of the things we have discussed:

- There is one God. Nothing can compare to God.
- God does not change, and nothing can change God.
- God is limitless and boundless. God cannot be measured.
- God knows everything. There is nothing God does not know.

- God is omnipresent. There is no place God does not exist.
- God created all things. God sustains all things.
- God needs nothing to exist. God does not need us.
- God transcends everything – time, space, matter. He is above and beyond all.
- God is perfect. God is perfect in His holiness and righteousness and goodness.
- God is eternal. He has always been and will forever be. He had no beginning and He will have no end.
- God is all powerful. Nothing can stand against His power. All power flows from God.
- God is in control of everything. Everything that happens is within His will.
- God is love. Even though God does not need man, He loves each of us so much that it seems to us that He needs us.
- God is so majestic and glorious that He is beyond man's imagination and comprehension.
- God is honest and faithful. He does not lie, and we can rest assured in all of His promises.
- God will forgive and forget all the sins of each and every person that comes to Him with faith, repentance, and the willingness to accept His gift of salvation. God's grace, mercy and love are infinite and limitless.

God, HE IS WHO HE IS – eternal, omnipotent, sovereign, holy - yet this majestic God desires to be your heavenly *Daddy*. The almighty God of the universe made you in His image (with free will) and wants to have a personal relationship with you. He desires to dwell within you, His child, with His Holy Spirit. That is mind-boggling! When you meditate upon these things, how can you not say, without any reservation, that your God is completely *worthy* of your worship and praise – a worship based on adoration, reverence, love, respect, and honor from your heart?

Look at the following "Worthiness Test". Take the time to carefully answer the questions. There is no grade or score to be determined. However, the test will give you an overall indication of how worthy God is to you and how much value you place on your personal relationship with the Lord God.

The Worthiness Test

Just how worthy is God to you personally? Answer these questions to help determine just how worthy you believe God is to you personally:

Question
How worthy is God of your time?

How worthy is God of your money?

How worthy is God of your faithfulness?

How much do you strive to be Christ-like?
     (Are you faithful around neighbors, friends and co-workers or just around fellow church members?)

How worthy is God of your praise and worship?

How often do you study God's Word?

How often do you pray to God?

Do you put forth a good effort to obey God?

Do you look for ways to serve God? Or do you serve only when asked? Or even avoid serving God?

How much do you sacrifice for Jesus Christ? How much do you "give up" in your service to Christ?

Are you willing to trust God always or only when things are going well?

Do you witness for Christ? Or only when it is comfortable? Or are you ashamed to talk about Christ? Do you look for opportunities?

Is Jesus Christ first in your life? Second? Third? Fourth?

Do you have great energy for God, great thoughts of God, great boldness for God, and great contentment in God? (1)

These are some tough questions that we must all consider if we truly believe all that the Bible says about God. The answers to these questions may cause you to grieve. That's good, because it is not too late to glorify God by showing Him, yourself and others that God is most worthy to you. Be determined to reflect God's worthiness in your daily living and service. Strive to have a closer personal relationship with God.

Appendices

Appendix A - The Attributes of God as Seen in Psalm 145

(See Day 6)

Psalm 145: A Praise to God's Attributes and Virtues

In the column on the left are the attributes of God that we have identified in Psalm 145. The column on the right identifies some of those things that we will do once we know God.

God's Attributes	Our Actions (When we know God)
Great, powerful, mighty	Exalt and extol Him
Worthy	Praise Him and His holy name
Glorious, splendor, majesty	Commend and meditate on His works
Abundant goodness	Speak, tell and proclaim Him and His works
Righteous	Look to Him
Gracious, compassionate	Celebrate Him
Good	Joyfully sing of Him
Slow to anger	Call on Him
Eternal	Fear Him
Faithful	Love Him
Near	Bow down before Him

Holy
Creative (awesome works)
Sovereign (His dominion)
Merciful (upholds, lifts up)
Personal (hears, watches over)
Just (destroys the wicked)

Appendix B – God's Love Letter to You

My Child…

> *You may not know me, but I know everything about you …Psalm 139:1*
>
> *I know when you sit down and when you rise up …Psalm 139:2*
>
> *I am familiar with all your ways …Psalm 139:3*
>
> *Even the very hairs on your head are numbered …Matthew 10:29-31*
>
> *For you were made in my image …Genesis 1:27*
>
> *In me you live and move and have your being …Acts 17:28*
>
> *For you are my offspring …Acts 17:28*
>
> *I knew you even before you were conceived …Jeremiah 1:4-5*
>
> *I chose you when I planned creation …Ephesians 1:11-12*
>
> *You were not a mistake, for all your days are written in my book …*
>
> *Psalm 139:15-16*
>
> *I determined the exact time of your birth and where you would live …*
>
> *Acts 17:26*
>
> *You are fearfully and wonderfully made …Psalm 139:14*
>
> *I knit you together in your mother's womb …Psalm 139:13*
>
> *And brought you forth on the day you were born …Psalm 71:6*

I have been misrepresented by those who don't know me ...John 8:41-44

I am not distant and angry, but am the complete expression of love ...

1 John 4:16

And it is my desire to lavish my love on you ...1 John 3:1

Simply because you are my child and I am your father ...1 John 3:1

I offer you more than your earthly father ever could ...Matthew 7:11

For I am the perfect father ...Matthew 5:48

Every good gift that you receive comes from my hand ...James 1:17

For I am your provider and I meet all your needs ...Matthew 6:31-33

My plan for your future has always been filled with hope ... Jeremiah 29:11

Because I love you with an everlasting love ...Jeremiah 31:3

My thoughts toward you are countless as the sand on the seashore...

Psalms 139:17-18

And I rejoice over you with singing ...Zephaniah 3:17

I will never stop doing good to you ...Jeremiah 32:40

For you are my treasured possession ...Exodus 19:5

I desire to establish you with all my heart and all my soul ... Jeremiah 32:41

And I want to show you great and marvelous things ...Jeremiah 33:3

If you seek me with all your heart, you will find me ...Deuteronomy 4:29

Delight in me and I will give you the desires of your heart ... Psalm 37:4

For it is I who gave you those desires ...Philippians 2:13

I am able to do more for you than you could possibly imagine ... Ephesians 3:20

For I am your greatest encourager ...2 Thessalonians 2:16-17

I am also the Father who comforts you in all your troubles ...

2 Corinthians 1:3-4

When you are brokenhearted, I am close to you ...Psalm 34:18

As a shepherd carries a lamb, I have carried you close to my heart ...

Isaiah 40:11

One day I will wipe away every tear from your eyes ...Revelation 21:3-4

And I'll take away all the pain you have suffered on this earth ...

Revelation 21:3-4

I am your Father, and I love you even as I love my son, Jesus ...John 17:23

For in Jesus, my love for you is revealed ...John 17:26

He is the exact representation of my being ...Hebrews 1:3

He came to demonstrate that I am for you, not against you ... Romans 8:31

And to tell you that I am not counting your sins ...2 Corinthians 5:18-19

Jesus died so that you and I could be reconciled ...2 Corinthians 5:18-19

His death was the ultimate expression of my love for you ...1 John 4:10

I gave up everything I loved that I might gain your love ...Romans 8:31-32

If you receive the gift of my son Jesus, you receive me ...1 John 2:23

And nothing will ever separate you from my love again ...Romans 8:38-39

Come home and I'll throw the biggest party heaven has ever seen ...Luke 15:7

I have always been Father, and will always be Father ...Ephesians 3:14-15

My question is... Will you be my child? ...John 1:12-13

I am waiting for you ...Luke 15:11-32

Love, Your Dad
Almighty God

Appendix C - The Divine Attributes Demonstrated in Jesus

The Scripture verses below depict how Jesus demonstrated and revealed the attributes of God that we have studied. Since there is one God – in three persons – each Person will possess these attributes.

Attribute	Scripture
Infinite and Divine Transcendence	Hebrews 1:1-3; Philippians 2:9
Eternal	John 8:54-59; Colossians 1:17; Hebrews 1:8
Self-existent and Self-sufficient	Colossians 1:16; Hebrews 1:3
Unchanging and Immutable	Hebrews 13:8
Glorious and Majestic	John 11:4; John 17:1-5; Matthew 17:1-8; 2 Peter 1:16
Omniscient and Wise	John 16:30, Colossians 2:3; Luke 10:22; 1 Corinthians 1:30
Omnipotent and Omnipresent	Matthew 14:25-27; 18:20; 28:6, 18-20; Luke 8:24-25; Mark 10:17; John 10:25

Faithful, Honest and Trustworthy	Hebrews 10:23; 1 Thessalonians 5:24
Patient	2 Peter 3:9, 15
Good and Compassionate	John 10:11-17; John 11:33-35; Mark 8:2-3
Just	John 5:22, 2 Timothy 2:4
Merciful and Gracious	Matthew 20:29-34; Luke 18:16; John 8:10-11; Hebrews 2:17
Love	Romans 5:8; Ephesians 3:18; John 15:12
Creative	John 1:3, Colossians 1:17
Worthy	John 5:23, Hebrews 1:6; Revelation 5:9, 12-14
Jealous and Wrathful	1 Corinthians 15:24-25; Revelation 19:15-18; John 2:12-16
Holy and Righteous	1 John 2:1; 1 Peter 3:18; 2 Peter 1:1; Hebrews 9:14
Sovereign	Colossians 2:10; Mark 2:10-11
Father	John 10:30, 36-38; 14:7; 17:5; Mark 5:34

Appendix D - The Divine Attributes Demonstrated in The Holy Spirit

The Scripture verses below depict how The Holy Spirit also demonstrates and reveals the attributes of God that we have studied. Since there is one God – in three persons – each Person will possess these attributes.

Attribute	Scripture
Infinite and Divine Transcendence	Acts 5:3-4 The Holy Spirit is called God.
	2 Cor 3:17-18 The Holy Spirit is called Lord, the Hebrew word kurios, which refers to the divine Being, Jehovah. (1)
	Romans 8:9
Eternal	Hebrews 9:14; John 14:16
Self-existent and Self-sufficient	
Unchanging and Immutable	
Glorious and Majestic	1 Peter 4:14
Omniscient and Wise	1 Corinthians 2:10-11; Ephesians 1:17; Isaiah 11:2; John 16:13; 2

	Peter 1:21
Omnipotent and Omnipresent	Psalm 139:7-10; Luke 1:35; Acts 8:39
Faithful, Honest and Trustworthy	John 16:13, 14:17, 15:26; 1 John 5:6-10; Romans 9:1
Patient	
Good and Compassionate	John 14:16, 26, 15:26, 16:7; Nehemiah 9:20
Just	Isaiah 4:4
Merciful and Gracious	Zechariah 12:10; Hebrews 10:29
Love	Romans 15:30; Galatians 5:22-23
Creative	Psalm 104:30; Job 33:4; Genesis 1:2
Worthy	Acts 5:1-9
Jealous and Wrathful	Acts 5:10-11
Holy and Righteous	Matthew 12:28-32; Mark 3:28-29; Luke 12:10; John 16:8
Sovereign	Acts 13:2; Acts 10:44; 1 Corinthians 12:1-11; Romans 8:27
Father	Matthew 10:20; Romans 8:12-17

Appendix E - Choice

In his book <u>Heaven</u>, Randy Alcorn has a very interesting comment: "The best of life on Earth is a glimpse of Heaven; the worst of life is a glimpse of Hell. For Christians, this present life is the closest they will come to Hell. For unbelievers, it is the closest they will come to Heaven." (1) That statement is worth pondering for a couple of moments. A person's life on earth has many great and wonderful things that God has provided. If the person is an unsaved sinner, he/she will never experience anything so good again. Likewise, his/her life on earth also has much heartache, pain and fear that are a result of man's sin. If the person is a redeemed child of God, he/she will never experience anything close to those again. It is a matter of choice for that person.

God has given each of us the freedom and the responsibility of CHOICE. Everyone over 30 probably remembers the game show "Let's Make a Deal", which was hosted by Monty Hall. Monty would offer a contestant a prize or they could choose what was behind Door #1, Door #2, or Door #3. It always amazed me how many people would give up a great prize that was theirs for the taking just for the right to trade for an unknown behind one of the doors. These contestants would know that there was a chance that they could lose out, but they always hoped for something better. Our lives and God's salvation are similar to this. *Grace* is a gift from God, but we must acknowledge and accept the gift. God has clearly revealed to us what the prize is. Yet so many decide to choose what is behind one of the doors. Satan, in the role of Monty Hall, does not care which door we choose, so long as we do not accept God's gift prize. Satan makes the doors inviting and appealing. If necessary, Satan will create and offer more doors – either to further entice us or to keep us from deciding to accept God's gift. He will do all he can to make the gift of grace seem unappealing or to make us feel unworthy to accept the gift. People choose not to accept the gift of grace and will choose one of the doors for any number of reasons. The problem is that they all lead to the same destination – hell.

Randy Alcorn states that our default destination is hell – *salvation by grace through faith* prevents the default from happening. Since **"all have sinned and fall short of the glory of God" (Romans 3:23)**, we must take that step of faith. *Grace* is a gift, but we must acknowledge and accept the gift. Not making a choice to accept Christ is the same as making a choice for one of Satan's doors. Two truths to remember:

"There is freedom to choose which side we will be on but no freedom to negotiate the results of the choice once it is made." (2)

References

A. A.W. Tozer, <u>The Knowledge of the Holy</u>, New York: HarperCollins, 1961.

B. Chip Ingram, <u>God: As He Longs for You to See Him</u>, Grand Rapids, Michigan: BakerBooks, 2004.

C. J. I. Packer, <u>Knowing God</u>, Downers Grove, Illinois: InterVarsity Press, 1973.

D. Arthur Pink, <u>The A. W. Pink Collection: The Attributes of God</u>, Rio, Wisconsin: Ages Software, Inc., 2005.

E. Dr. Charles Stanley, "A Passion to Obey God", the June 4, 2003 sermon from the audio archives on the InTouch Ministries Website

F. Erwin W. Lutzer, <u>Seven Reasons Why You Can Trust The Bible</u>, Chicago: Moody Press, 1998.

G. Josh McDowell, <u>The New Evidence That Demands a Verdict</u>, Nashville: Thomas Nelson Publishers, 1999.

H. Dr. Adrian Rogers, <u>When We Say "Father"</u>, a sermon from the website "Love Worth Finding"

I. January 2006 issue, InTouch magazine, "Those Who Seek the Lord Lack No Good Thing"

J. Randy Alcorn, <u>Heaven</u>, Wheaton, Illinois: Tyndale House Publishers, Inc., 2004.

K. Dr. Charles Stanley, "The Greatness of God", the April 15, 2005 sermon from the audio archives on the InTouch Ministries Website

L. William Evans, <u>What Every Christian Should Believe</u>, Chicago: Moody Press, 2001.

M. Bobby Linkous, Pastor at Shadowbrook Baptist Church, Suwanee, GA, Sermon handout

N. R. C. Sproul, "Receiving God's Forgiveness", a sermon on the Ligonier Ministries website on 2/28/06.

O. Grant R. Jeffrey, <u>Creation: Remarkable Evidence of God's Design</u>, Toronto: Frontier Research Publications, 2003.

P. Dr. Charles Stanley, "The Patience of God", the November 23, 2004 sermon from the audio archives on the InTouch Ministries Website

Q. Dr. Adrian Rogers, <u>Why Do I Exist?</u>, March 9, 2006 sermon from the website "Love Worth Finding"

R. Dr. Charles Stanley, <u>Seeking His Face: A Daily Devotional</u>, Nashville: Thomas Nelson Publishers, 2002.

S. Rick Warren, <u>The Purpose Driven Life</u>, Grand Rapids, Michigan: Zondervan, 2002.

T. April 2006 issue, InTouch magazine, "Because He Lives: Why Does the Resurrection Matter?"

U. Dr. Charles Stanley, "The Ten Commandments", the November 14-16 sermons from the audio archives on the InTouch Ministries Website

V. R. A. Torrey, <u>What the Bible Teaches</u>, New Kensington, PA: Whitaker House, 1996.

W. Robert Jeffress, "Healing Words for Hurting Hearts", August 16, 2006 sermon from the Pathway to Victory Website

Booklet   Cover (Quotes in order)
          1.   A, p. 1
          2.   B, p. 30
          3.   C, p. 19
          4.   B, p. 30
          5.   A, p. 2
          6.   A, p. 3
          7.   C, p. 17

Day 1   Introduction
1.   H
2.   B, cover
3.   C, p. 27-31

Day 2   Why Is It Important to Truly Know God?
1.   A, p. 1
2.   B, p. 31
3.   B, p. 47

Day 3   Problems with Custom-Ordered Gods

Day 4   Where Can I Find the True God?
1.   F, p.51
2.   F, p. 51
3.   F, p. 47
4.   F, p. 45
5.   F, p. 46
6.   G, p. 9
7.   G, p. 61

Day 5   Knowing God Starts with Seeking God
1.   I, p. 7
2.   I, p. 8

Day 6   The Divine Attributes of God
1.   A, p. 12
2.   A, p. 16
3.   A, p. 15
4.   A, p. 15

Day 7   The Holy Trinity
1.   A, p. 22
2.   A, p. 23

Day 8   Infinite and Divine Transcendence
1.   A, p. 69
2.   A, p. 44-45
3.   A, p. 45

Day 9   Eternal
1.   A, p. 39
2.   A, p. 40
3.   A, p. 47

Day 10   Self-Existent and Self-Sufficient

	1. A, p. 35
	2. A, p. 35
Day 11	Unchanging and Immutable
	1. C, pages 76-81
	2. C, p. 77
	3. D, also C, p. 77
	4. C, p. 77
	5. C, p. 78
	6. C, p. 79
	7. C, p. 79
	8. C, p. 80
	9. A, p. 53
Day 12	Glorious and Majestic
	1. C, p. 88
	2. C, p. 88
	3. K
	4. C, p. 88
	5. C, p. 89
Day 13	Omniscient and Wise
	1. A, p. 60
	2. A, p. 60-61
	3. B, p. 128
	4. B, p. 129
	5. C, p. 106
	6. B, p. 139
	7. B, p. 141
Day 14	Omnipotence and Omnipresence
	1. A, p. 67
	2. A, p. 76
Day 15	Faithful, Honest and Trustworthy
	1. B, p. 221-222
Day 16	Patient
	1. P, much of Day 16 is taken from this sermon by Dr. Charles Stanley
Day 17	Good and Compassionate
	1. A, p. 82
	2. A, p. 84

	3.	A, p. 82
Day 18	Just	
	1.	C, p. 143
	2.	A, p. 89
Day 19	Merciful and Gracious	
	1.	A, p. 90
	2.	A, p. 93
	3.	A, p. 92
	4.	N, part of Day 18 is based on this sermon
Day 20	Love	
	1.	A, p. 102
	2.	B, p. 181
Day 21	Creativity	
	1.	O, facts taken from throughout the book
Day 22	Worthy	
Day 23	Jealous	
	1.	C, p. 160
	2.	C, p. 160
	3.	C, p. 160
Day 24	Holy and Righteous	
	1.	L, p. 73
	2.	A, p. 104
	3.	A, p. 105
	4.	D, p. 37
	5.	D, p. 37-38
	6.	D, p. 39-40
Day 25	Sovereign	
	1.	W, this quote and other thoughts are taken from this message
	2.	A, p. 111
Day 26	Father	
	1.	C, p. 200
	2.	C, p. 201
	3.	C, p. 201
	4.	C, p. 203
	5.	C, p. 203
	6.	C, p. 207

Appendix E – Choice

        1.   J, p. 28
        2.   A, p. 112

Printed in the United States
123202LV00004B/1-141/P